EXECUTIVE SUMMARY

This review by the Department of Justice (Department) Office of the Inspector General (OIG) examined the impact of the Bureau of Alcohol, Tobacco, Firearms and Explosives' (ATF) implementation of Project Gunrunner on the illicit trafficking of guns from the United States to Mexico.

Violence associated with organized crime and drug trafficking in Mexico is widespread, resulting in tens of thousands of deaths. In part because Mexican law severely restricts gun ownership, drug traffickers have turned to the United States as a primary source of weapons, and these drug traffickers routinely smuggle guns from the United States into Mexico. The criminal organizations responsible for smuggling guns to Mexico are typically also involved in other criminal enterprises, such as drug trafficking, human trafficking, and cash smuggling. This requires ATF to work with other federal entities, as well as with state and local law enforcement partners, in sharing intelligence, coordinating law enforcement activities, and building cases that can be prosecuted.

To help combat firearms trafficking into Mexico, ATF began Project Gunrunner as a pilot project in Laredo, Texas, in 2005 and expanded it as a national initiative in 2006. Project Gunrunner is also part of the Department's broader Southwest Border Initiative, which seeks to reduce cross-border drug and firearms trafficking and the high level of violence associated with these activities on both sides of the border.

In June 2007, ATF published a strategy document, *Southwest Border Initiative: Project Gunrunner* (Gunrunner strategy), outlining four key components to Project Gunrunner: the expansion of gun tracing in Mexico, international coordination, domestic activities, and intelligence. In implementing Project Gunrunner, ATF has focused resources in its four Southwest border field divisions. In addition, ATF has made firearms trafficking to Mexico a top ATF priority nationwide.

The OIG conducted this review to evaluate the effectiveness of ATF's implementation of Project Gunrunner. Our review examined ATF's enforcement and regulatory programs related to the Southwest border and Mexico, ATF's effectiveness in developing and sharing firearms trafficking intelligence and information, the number and prosecutorial outcomes of ATF's Project Gunrunner investigations, ATF's coordination with U.S. and Mexican law enforcement partners, ATF's traces of Mexican "crime guns," and challenges that ATF faces in coordinating efforts to combat firearms trafficking with Mexico.[1]

RESULTS OF THE OIG REVIEW

ATF's Expanded Efforts in Support of Project Gunrunner

To assess the impact of Project Gunrunner, we first examined data on ATF's performance in tracing guns, conducting criminal investigations, conducting compliance inspections of gun dealers in the region, and referring leads to ATF's criminal enforcement personnel for action. We compared data in these areas from fiscal year (FY) 2004 through FY 2006 (3 years prior to ATF's implementation of Project Gunrunner), with data from FY 2007 through FY 2009 (the initial 3 full years of Project Gunrunner).

The data showed that since ATF's implementation of Project Gunrunner, ATF has increased its:

1. Traces of seized firearms from Mexico and from the Southwest border – Trace requests initiated in Mexico rose from 1 percent of all Mexico and U.S. trace requests prior to Project Gunrunner to 8 percent during Project Gunrunner.

2. Project Gunrunner cases initiated, cases referred for prosecution to U.S. Attorneys' Offices (USAO), and defendants referred for prosecution for firearms trafficking-related offenses – ATF increased the number of Project Gunrunner cases it initiated by 109 percent and increased the number of those cases it referred to USAOs by 54 percent.[2] The number of defendants ATF referred for prosecution increased by 37 percent.

---

[1] According to ATF, crime guns are guns that were "recovered by law enforcement that were used in a crime, were suspected to have been used in a crime, or were recovered in relation to a crime." Mark Kraft, "Firearms Trafficking 101 or Where Do Crime Guns Come From?," *United States Attorneys' Bulletin* (January 2002).

[2] ATF considers any investigation conducted nationwide to be a "Project Gunrunner case" if it involves firearms trafficking or violent crime and has a connection to the Southwest border. This could include cases also coded as gang-related or as another type of case. Our discussion of Project Gunrunner cases in this report is based on ATF data that meets this definition.

U.S. Department of Justice   ii
Office of the Inspector General
Evaluation and Inspections Division

3. Gun dealer compliance inspections conducted on the Southwest border, inspection hours worked by Southwest border field division inspectors, and inspection finding referrals made to ATF's criminal enforcement personnel for subsequent action – ATF increased the number of gun dealer compliance inspections along the Southwest Border by 133 percent and increased the number of compliance inspection hours worked by 102 percent. The total number of referrals ATF Industry Operations personnel made to ATF criminal enforcement personnel increased by 47 percent.

In addition to its increased program activities described above, ATF implemented a Gunrunner Impact Team initiative that increased the number of gun dealer compliance inspections conducted and cases initiated within the Houston Field Division area. Under this initiative, ATF deployed 100 agents, investigators, and support staff to the Houston Field Division for 120 days. ATF reported that the team conducted over 1,000 inspections of gun dealers and generated investigative leads leading to the seizure of over 400 firearms.

Despite the increased ATF activity associated with Project Gunrunner, we found that significant weaknesses in ATF's implementation of Project Gunrunner undermine its effectiveness.

ATF Firearms Trafficking Intelligence and Information

We found that ATF does not systematically and consistently exchange intelligence with its Mexican and some U.S. partner agencies. In addition, some ATF field agents reported that they do not find investigative leads provided to them by ATF's Field Intelligence Groups to be timely and usable. We also determined that intelligence personnel in ATF's Southwest border field divisions do not routinely share firearms trafficking intelligence with each other. ATF could better implement its Border Liaison Program to improve information sharing and coordination between its U.S. and its Mexico personnel.

The success of Project Gunrunner depends, in part, on ATF's sharing intelligence with its Mexican and U.S. partner agencies, including the Drug Enforcement Administration (DEA) and the Department of Homeland Security's (DHS) Immigration and Customs Enforcement (ICE). Although ATF has shared some strategic intelligence products with each of its partner agencies, it is not doing so systematically and consistently. ATF does share tactical intelligence regularly with the DEA and DHS's Customs and Border Protection (CBP).[3] However, ATF has not provided Mexican law enforcement with intelligence it requested on firearms trafficking patterns and trends, including trafficking routes and distribution points where guns are crossing into Mexico.

We also found that while reports of multiple sales of handguns produce timely, actionable investigative leads for ATF, the lack of a reporting requirement for multiple sales of long guns – which have become the cartels' weapons of choice – hinders ATF's ability to disrupt the flow of illegal weapons into Mexico.

In addition, when ATF obtains or generates intelligence, its Southwest border field divisions' intelligence structure is not consistently using that information to provide effective investigative leads for field agents to pursue. Specifically, the Field Intelligence Groups of ATF's Southwest border field divisions are not forwarding leads that are timely, that are developed beyond what field agents state they can do themselves or that contribute to investigations. Intelligence personnel in the Southwest border field divisions also lack a common understanding of how to develop and screen intelligence accurately to meet the requirements of enforcement groups. They do not operate under consistent guidelines or clear criteria that specify the most useful types of investigative leads. Additionally, ATF managers must rely on two separate ATF case management systems and do not have an automated process to track the status, monitor the outcomes, or evaluate the effectiveness of investigative leads provided to agents.

We also found no routine sharing of firearms trafficking-related information and techniques between ATF intelligence personnel in Southwest border locations and in the ATF Mexico Country Office. Intelligence coordination, when it does happen, occurs at the supervisory level, but non-supervisory intelligence personnel lack a method to regularly share information, best practices, and analytical techniques that they told us would be useful to them.

One illustration of the lack of information sharing is ATF's weak implementation of its Border Liaison Program. ATF's 2007 Gunrunner

---

[3] ATF defines tactical intelligence as information produced to support operations or that relates to the specific time, date, nature, and other details of events. Strategic intelligence is defined as information required for the formulation of policy and plans at the regional, national, and international levels. Strategic intelligence differs primarily from tactical intelligence in level of use but may also vary in scope and detail.

strategy identifies ATF's border liaisons as "the front line" of Project Gunrunner. However, we found that the border liaisons' roles are not well defined and their activities in Mexico are not well coordinated.

ATF Investigative Focus

Firearms traffickers also participate in other criminal activity, such as drug trafficking, human trafficking, and cash smuggling. The complexity of their operations requires ATF to work closely with the government of Mexico, other U.S. federal agencies and departments, and state and local law enforcement partners.

Yet, we found weaknesses in how ATF implemented Project Gunrunner as a multi-agency effort. Although, as noted above, ATF has increased some program activities during Project Gunrunner, ATF's focus remains largely on inspections of gun dealers and investigations of straw purchasers, rather than on higher-level traffickers, smugglers, and the ultimate recipients of the trafficked guns.[4]

For example, we found that 68 percent of Project Gunrunner cases are single-defendant cases, and some ATF managers discourage field personnel from conducting the types of complex conspiracy investigations that target higher-level members of trafficking rings. Federal prosecutors told us that directing the efforts of Project Gunrunner toward building larger, multi-defendant conspiracy cases would better disrupt trafficking organizations.

Moreover, although ATF has had a long-stated intent to make fuller use of the resources of the Department's Organized Crime Drug Enforcement Task Force (OCDETF) Program to conduct more complex conspiracy investigations, it has not done so. This is in part due to ATF's focus on conducting fast investigations and also due to misunderstandings among ATF field personnel about what kinds of cases are eligible for OCDETF and whether OCDETF cases are counted as Project Gunrunner cases by ATF's internal performance metrics.

---

[4] According to ATF, a "straw purchase" occurs when the actual buyer of a firearm uses another person, "the straw purchaser," to execute the paperwork necessary to purchase a firearm from a gun dealer. The actual buyer is often prohibited from purchasing the gun. The straw purchaser violates federal law by making a false statement with respect to the information required to be kept in the gun dealer's records. According to ATF, straw purchasing is one of the most frequent methods used to illegally acquire guns.

U.S. Department of Justice   v
Office of the Inspector General
Evaluation and Inspections Division

Because there is no federal firearms trafficking statute, ATF must use a wide variety of other statutes to combat firearms trafficking. However, cases brought under these statutes are difficult to prove and do not carry stringent penalties – particularly for straw purchasers of guns. As a result, we found that USAOs are less likely to accept and prosecute Project Gunrunner cases. And when these cases are prosecuted and convictions obtained, Federal Sentencing Guidelines categorize straw-purchasing-related offenses as lesser crimes.

Multi-Agency Coordination Issues

We also found that ATF and ICE do not work together effectively on investigations of firearms trafficking to Mexico, and therefore ATF's Project Gunrunner cases do not benefit from ICE's intelligence and prosecutorial options. ATF and ICE rarely conduct joint investigations of firearms trafficking to Mexico, do not consistently notify each other of their firearms trafficking cases, and do not consistently coordinate their investigative work with each other.

A memorandum of understanding (MOU) signed by ATF and ICE in 2009 sought to foster better coordination, but we found that ATF and ICE agents and supervisors misunderstood the intent of the MOU or were unaware of it. Consequently, adequate coordination between ATF and ICE is still lacking in those areas of concurrent jurisdiction that are described in the MOU.

Mexican Crime Gun Tracing

Despite the increased activity related to Project Gunrunner, ATF is not using intelligence effectively to identify and target firearms trafficking organizations operating along the Southwest border and in Mexico. Moreover, ATF's expansion of its automated system (eTrace) to trace guns seized in Mexico has yielded very limited information of intelligence value.

According to ATF's June 2007 Gunrunner strategy, tracing guns seized in Mexico is the "cornerstone" of Project Gunrunner. Tracing seized guns to the gun dealer which sold the gun to the first retail purchaser is a crucial source of information in ATF's investigations of firearms trafficking. Gun tracing also helps ATF identify firearm traffickers operating in the United States and in Mexico and can provide intelligence in the form of patterns and trends in gun smuggling.

However, ATF has been unable to expand gun tracing throughout Mexico. A June 2009 Government Accountability Office report estimated that trace data was submitted to ATF on less than a quarter of the guns seized in Mexico. Further, most trace requests that are submitted to ATF from Mexico are considered "unsuccessful" because of missing or improperly entered gun data.[5] Although ATF has provided Mexican law enforcement with training in firearms identification, we found the percentage of total trace requests that succeed has declined since the start of Project Gunrunner. Moreover, few of the traces that do succeed generate usable investigative leads because guns submitted for tracing often were seized by Mexican officials years before the trace requests were submitted. In such cases, the time at which a gun was transferred illegally may be outside the statute of limitations and charges cannot be brought against those responsible.

We determined that Mexican law enforcement authorities do not view gun tracing as an important investigative tool for them. One reason for this is that ATF's trace results do not include the detailed investigative information on U.S. citizens that Mexican officials have requested (such as the criminal histories of those who may be involved in firearms trafficking). This information must be requested separately from the trace results. Some ATF officials also told us that ATF has not adequately communicated the value of gun tracing to Mexican officials. Consequently, Mexican law enforcement officials view gun tracing as merely a tool that ATF uses to further its own investigations. The Mexican officials did not see the long-term benefits of gun tracing in reducing the flow of illegal guns to Mexico by targeting the sources of these guns and the organizations that traffic them on both sides of the U.S.-Mexico border.

---

[5] ATF stated that its common definition of a "successful trace" is a trace that provides any additional historical or identifying information concerning the firearm beyond the original information submitted in the trace request. However, ATF staff provided us different definitions of a successful trace, such as one that identifies the first purchaser. We define a successful trace as one that identifies the gun dealer who originally sold the weapon because that is the minimum result that can provide ATF with usable intelligence information.

According to ATF National Tracing Center data, an invalid serial number was the most common reason for unsuccessful traces from Mexico. However, crime gun traces can be unsuccessful for many other reasons. For example, the requester may not have provided a manufacturer or importer, or the gun may have been manufactured prior to 1968 when the *Gun Control Act* was enacted and thus no records were required.

U.S. Department of Justice   vii
Office of the Inspector General
Evaluation and Inspections Division

ATF Coordination Challenges in Mexico

<u>Resource and Coordination Difficulties</u>

Our review found that because of a lack of resources, ATF has been unable to fully meet Mexican government needs for support under Project Gunrunner. For example, ATF has been unable to provide key training and support requested by the government of Mexico. Further, the process of exchanging law enforcement investigative information between ATF and the government of Mexico is cumbersome, and ATF has a substantial backlog in responding to requests for information from Mexican authorities, which has hindered coordination between ATF and Mexican law enforcement. ATF also has been unable to recruit sufficient qualified staff to fill positions in the Mexico Country Office and does not offer incentives to attract and retain qualified staff there.

U.S. officials told us they face multiple unique challenges in coordinating with Mexican law enforcement officials. For example, U.S. officials we interviewed in Mexico stated that there is a lack of coordination among various Mexican law enforcement agencies and that ATF has no single counterpart that it can interact with in coordinating firearms trafficking investigations. Internal coordination problems within the government of Mexico require that ATF deal separately with multiple agencies there, which has slowed information sharing. ATF's effort to improve coordination by embedding a representative of the Mexico Attorney General's office in ATF's Phoenix Field Division on a trial basis has improved ATF's access to Mexican law enforcement's information.

<u>Lack of an Integrated Project Gunrunner Approach</u>

An overarching problem our review found was that ATF has not integrated the Project Gunrunner activities of its four Southwest border divisions and ATF's Mexico Country Office into a coordinated approach. ATF's Project Gunrunner strategies and plans do not effectively address coordination, joint operations and investigations, or information sharing across these units. We believe this has been a contributing factor in several other shortfalls addressed in this review, including the ineffective intelligence and information sharing within ATF, unclear roles for border liaison personnel, inadequate and disparate staffing in Mexico, failure to focus on complex conspiracy firearms trafficking investigations, and poor coordination with other U.S. and Mexican law enforcement agencies.

U.S. Department of Justice   viii
Office of the Inspector General
Evaluation and Inspections Division

In September 2010, after our draft report was issued, ATF disseminated to field personnel and International Affairs Office staff a strategy, entitled "Project Gunrunner – A Cartel Focused Strategy," that responds to many of the issues identified in this report. We refer to this strategy at various places in this report. However, it is not clear when, or how, this strategy will be fully implemented.

Recommendations

In this report, we make 15 recommendations to ATF to help improve its efforts in combating firearms trafficking from the United States to Mexico. For example, we recommend that ATF improve its generation of investigative leads to agents working on Project Gunrunner and improve its intelligence sharing within ATF and with its U.S. and Mexican partners, and that ATF focus on more complex conspiracy cases to dismantle firearms trafficking rings. To improve coordination between ATF and ICE, we recommend that ATF provide specific guidance to require better coordination with ICE in accordance with the agencies' memorandum of understanding. We also recommend that ATF work with Mexican law enforcement officials to determine the causes of unsuccessful Mexican crime gun traces and to improve the rate of successful traces. We also recommend that ATF consider implementing incentives to attract qualified staff to its Mexico Country Office. In addition, to provide a coordinated approach to ATF's implementation of Project Gunrunner, we recommend that ATF implement a plan to integrate the activities of the Mexico Country Office and Southwest Border field divisions.

U.S. Department of Justice   ix
Office of the Inspector General
Evaluation and Inspections Division

U.S. Department of Justice
Office of the Inspector General
Evaluation and Inspections Division

TABLE OF CONTENTS

U.S. Department of Justice
Office of the Inspector General
Evaluation and Inspections Division

BACKGROUND

Introduction

Mexican drug trafficking organizations (cartels) are a significant organized crime threat, both to the United States and in Mexico. According to the Department of Justice's (Department) 2010 National Drug Threat Assessment, Mexican cartels present the single greatest drug trafficking threat to the United States and are active in every region of the United States. Mexican cartels use violence to control lucrative drug trafficking corridors along the Southwest border, through which drugs flow north into the United States, while guns and cash flow south to Mexico.[6]

From December 2006 through July 2010, the Mexican government reported almost 30,000 deaths in Mexico resulting from organized crime and drug trafficking, with 9,635 murders in 2009 alone. In its fiscal year (FY) 2010 to FY 2016 strategic plan, the Bureau of Alcohol, Tobacco, Firearms and Explosives (ATF) reported that Mexico's drug traffickers have turned aggressively to the United States as a source of guns and routinely smuggle guns from the United States into Mexico. This is, in part, because Mexican law severely restricts gun ownership.

In 2009, ATF reported to Congress that about 90 percent of the guns recovered in Mexico that ATF has traced were initially sold in the United States.[7] The Southwest border states – Texas, California, Arizona, and to a lesser extent, New Mexico – are primary sources of guns used by Mexican drug cartels. The growing crime rate in Mexico, and fears that the violence will spill over into the United States, have led to efforts by U.S. and Mexican authorities to attempt to curb firearms trafficking.

---

[6] Congressional Research Service, *Mexico's Drug-Related Violence,* CRS Report R40582 (May 27, 2009).

[7] William McMahon, Deputy Assistant Director for Field Operations, ATF, before the Committee on Homeland Security Subcommittee on Border, Maritime, and Global Counterterrorism, U.S. House of Representatives, concerning "Combating Border Violence: The Role of Interagency Coordination in Investigations" (July 16, 2009), homeland.house.gov/Hearings/index.asp?ID=205 (accessed August 25, 2010). However, in September 2010, in response to a draft of this report ATF told the OIG that the 90-percent figure cited to Congress could be misleading because it applied only to the small portion of Mexican crime guns that are traced. ATF could not provide updated information on the percentage of traced Mexican crime guns that were sourced to (that is, found to be manufactured in or imported through) the United States.

ATF is one of the primary U.S. law enforcement agencies combating firearms trafficking from the United States to Mexico. ATF enforces federal firearms laws and also regulates the sale of guns by the firearms industry under the *Gun Control Act of 1968*. ATF is the only federal agency authorized to license and inspect gun dealers to ensure they comply with laws governing the sale, transfer, possession, and transport of guns.[8] ATF is also responsible for tracing guns by researching manufacturer and gun dealer data to identify the original purchasers of guns that are subsequently "recovered by law enforcement that were used in a crime, were suspected to have been used in a crime, or were recovered in relation to a crime."[9] These guns are termed "crime guns."

Project Gunrunner

Project Gunrunner, ATF's national initiative to stem firearms trafficking to Mexico, is part of the Department's broader Southwest Border Initiative, which combines the Department's law enforcement components in a concerted effort to reduce cross-border drug and weapons trafficking and the high level of violence associated with these activities. ATF began Project Gunrunner in 2005 as a pilot project in Laredo, Texas, and expanded it into a national program in 2006.[10]

ATF established five main objectives for Project Gunrunner:

1. Investigate individuals responsible for illicit firearms trafficking along the Southwest border.
2. Coordinate with U.S. and Mexican law enforcement along the border in firearms cases and violent crime.
3. Train U.S. and Mexican law enforcement officials to identify firearms traffickers.
4. Provide outreach education to gun dealers.
5. Trace all guns to identify firearms traffickers, trends, patterns, and networks.

---

[8] In this report, the term "gun dealers" refers to federal firearms licensees who are licensed through ATF to manufacture, import, or deal in guns.

[9] Mark Kraft, "Firearms Trafficking 101 or Where Do Crime Guns Come From?," *United States Attorneys' Bulletin* (January 2002).

[10] The exact inception date of Project Gunrunner is unclear. According to an April 28, 2009, ATF news release, Project Gunrunner began in 2005. However, ATF officials told us that they consider April 2006 the official implementation date of Project Gunrunner.

ATF's primary geographic focus for Project Gunrunner is in the four ATF field divisions that provide coverage for the almost 2,000-mile border with Mexico. These four field divisions are headquartered in Houston, Dallas, Phoenix, and Los Angeles.

The first three of ATF's five objectives listed above refer directly to Mexico or to the Southwest border. The remaining two objectives (Objectives 4 and 5) are more national in scope because the sources of firearms trafficked to Mexico are nationwide.

Figure 1 illustrates the Southwest border region as defined by ATF.[11]

Figure 1: The Southwest Border Region, as Defined by ATF

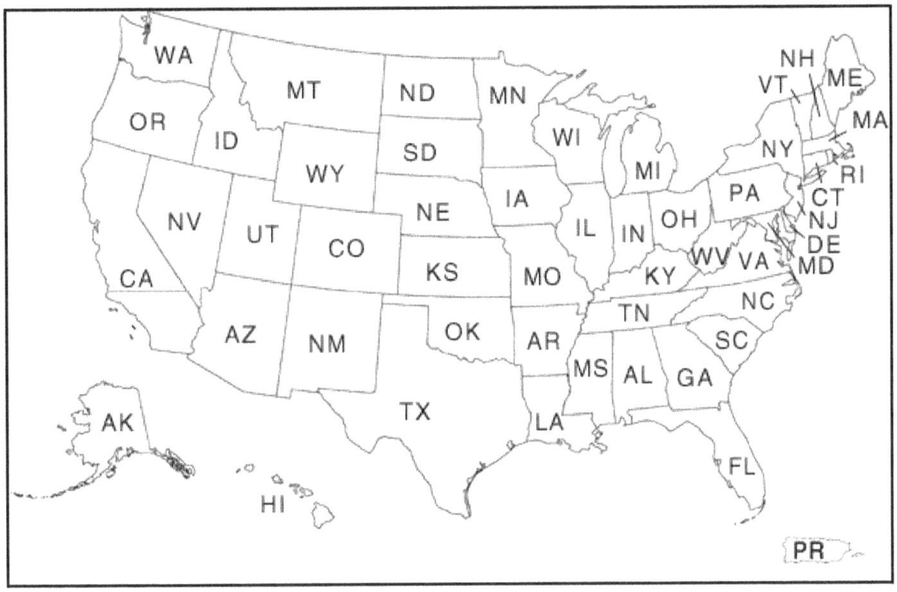

Source: OIG.

In June 2007, ATF published a strategy document, *Southwest Border Initiative: Project Gunrunner* (Gunrunner strategy), which outlined four key components: the expansion of ATF's crime gun tracing system (eTrace), international strategy, domestic strategy, and intelligence. We briefly describe each of those key components below.

Expansion of eTrace. ATF emphasized tracing crime guns as the "cornerstone" of Project Gunrunner and identified the expansion of eTrace into Mexico as an integral element of the project. The strategy incorporated ATF's plan to deploy eTrace in Mexico and established key roles for ATF's

---

[11] Although Oklahoma is a part of the Dallas Field Division, it is typically not considered a part of the Southwest border.

Mexico Country Office, National Tracing Center, and Violent Crime Analysis Branch in collecting and analyzing trace data from Mexico. We discuss eTrace further in the section, "Gun Tracing and eTrace," below.

International Component. The international component of the Gunrunner strategy addressed the coordination of ATF's activities in Mexico, including with the Department of State and the government of Mexico, and coordination between ATF's Mexico Country Office and its Southwest border divisions. Further, the document defined ATF's roles in providing, or helping to provide, technologies, equipment, information, and training to Mexican federal law enforcement.

Domestic Component. The domestic component of the strategy focused ATF resources in its four Southwest border field divisions. The strategy recognized a broader need to make firearms trafficking associated with crime guns seized along the Southwest border a top ATF priority nationwide. Additionally, the strategy document outlined ATF's approach to using criminal investigations and regulatory inspections to target the illicit flow of firearms to the Southwest border and into Mexico. It also directed the expansion of ATF's participation in other task force organizations, internal and external to the Department.

Intelligence Component. ATF's strategy document stated that Project Gunrunner intelligence must be "real time" to be effective, and it described how intelligence must flow within ATF and to and from its domestic and Mexican partners. The document also assigned responsibilities within ATF for oversight and coordination of ATF's intelligence and information sharing activities. The strategy established ATF's Gun Desk at the Drug Enforcement Administration (DEA) led El Paso Intelligence Center (EPIC) as ATF's clearinghouse for intelligence and investigative information.[12]

In its FY 2010 to FY 2016 strategic plan, ATF reiterated that Project Gunrunner is its primary enforcement initiative to stem the trafficking of illegal weapons across the U.S. border into Mexico and to reduce gun-driven violence on both sides of the border.[13]

---

[12] In addition to the DEA and ATF, 19 other agencies are represented at EPIC, including the Federal Bureau of Investigation (FBI), Immigration and Customs Enforcement, Customs and Border Protection, and state and local law enforcement. See U.S. Department of Justice Office of the Inspector General, *Review of the Drug Enforcement Administration's El Paso Intelligence Center,* Evaluation and Inspections Report I-2010-005 (June 2010), for more information.

[13] Appendix I provides a timeline of key events related to Project Gunrunner.

Project Gunrunner Budget

Initially, Project Gunrunner had no dedicated funding within ATF's budget. ATF funded all of the initiative's operations out of its general appropriation. As ATF expanded the initiative in response to the increased violence in Mexico and concern over firearms trafficking into Mexico, ATF began seeking dedicated funds for Project Gunrunner, starting with its FY 2008 budget request. In FY 2009, ATF received $21.9 million to support and expand Project Gunrunner. This included $5.9 million in ATF's FY 2009 appropriation for Project Gunrunner, $10 million in March 2009 from the *American Recovery and Reinvestment Act of 2009* (Recovery Act), and an additional $6 million in June of that year. Under Public Law No. 111-230 (2010), Emergency Border Security Supplemental Appropriations, ATF received an additional $37.5 million for the continued expansion of Project Gunrunner in FY 2010.[14]

Project Gunrunner Staffing

ATF Staffing on the Southwest Border. The number of ATF staff dedicated to Project Gunrunner in the four Southwest border field divisions has increased steadily since FY 2006, but most notably from FY 2008 through FY 2009 (Figure 2).[15] In 2006, ATF had 84 Special Agents assigned to Project Gunrunner. By June 2010, the number had increased 167 percent to 224 agents. The number of Industry Operations Investigators increased even more sharply, from 15 in 2006 to 165 in 2010, a 1,000-percent increase. Project Gunrunner staff also includes individuals in other job categories, such as Intelligence Research Specialists and Investigative Analysts, depicted in Figure 2 as "other." As of June 2010, the number of agents assigned to Project Gunrunner represented 50 percent of all agents in the four Southwest border field divisions, and the number of Industry Operations Investigators represented 92 percent of the

---

[14] Pub. L. No. 111-230 was signed into law on August 13, 2010. The bill provided $600 million in emergency supplemental appropriations for FY 2010 to secure the Southwest border and enhance federal border protection, law enforcement, and counternarcotics activities. The $37.5 million allocated to ATF was part of $196 million allocated to the Department.

[15] Because Project Gunrunner is a national initiative, additional personnel in locations beyond the Southwest border work Project Gunrunner cases. For example, a case involving firearms trafficking to Mexico that originates in the Midwest would be pursued by ATF agents there under Project Gunrunner.

---

investigators there.[16] Appendix II provides a description of the general duties for ATF staff.

Figure 2: Dedicated Project Gunrunner
Southwest Border Staff in the United States, by Fiscal Year

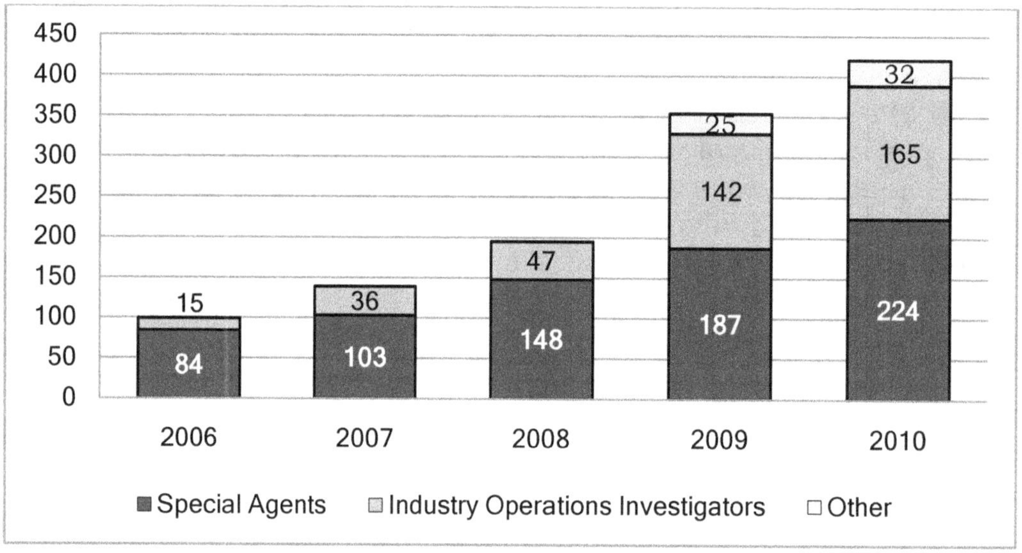

Note: ATF could not provide the numbers of staff in the "other" category prior to 2008.

Source: ATF data.

ATF Staffing in Mexico. Project Gunrunner is also supported by ATF's Mexico Country Office staff. The ATF Mexico Country Office is headed by an ATF Attaché and staffed by Assistant Attachés who are agents. At the time of our site visit in March 2010, the staff also included one Intelligence Research Specialist, one agent on temporary duty (TDY), and several Foreign Service Nationals (Mexican nationals employed by ATF). The staff of the Mexico Country Office coordinates with Mexican law enforcement agencies and facilitates information sharing; trains Mexican law enforcement personnel on subjects such as properly identifying and tracing weapons and conducting firearms trafficking and explosives investigations; and collects

---

[16] The most recent staffing increases were funded by several sources, including: (1) the Recovery Act, which provided 37 additional positions; (2) the President's global war on terror funding; and (3) ATF's FY 2009 appropriation. We described ATF's allocation of those funds in the report entitled *Interim Review of ATF's Project Gunrunner,* Evaluation and Inspections Report I-2009-006 (September 2009).

information on seized crime guns and explosives, which they forward to ATF personnel in the United States for investigation.[17]

As of June 2010, ATF had 13 staff assigned to the Mexico Country Office. Seven worked in the U.S. Embassy in Mexico City, and the other six worked in the U.S. Consulates in Monterrey (three), Tijuana (two), and Juarez (one).[18] Of the 13 staff, 8 were on permanent assignments to Mexico, and 5 were on TDY.

In its FY 2010 budget authorization, ATF received funding to increase the number of staff in Mexico. In September 2010, in response to a draft of this report, ATF stated that, since we completed fieldwork for this review, it had added 8 additional positions in Mexico – 3 in Mexico City, 2 each in Guadalajara and Hermosillo, and 1 in Merida, for a total of 18 authorized positions in Mexico. However, according to ATF, as of September 2010 only two of the eight new positions had been filled and recruitment and selection were under way for the remaining six positions. ATF also noted that even when it makes selections for personnel in Mexico, those personnel may not report to Mexico until their positions are "accredited" by the Mexican Secretariat of Foreign Relations, which had not occurred for the six open positions. Also, in September 2010 ATF reported that there were eight Foreign Service Nationals in the Mexico Country Office.

ATF's Enforcement, Regulatory, and Intelligence Functions

As described below, Project Gunrunner involves the ATF firearms trafficking enforcement, regulatory, and intelligence functions. We also discuss laws governing firearms trafficking and the private sale of guns.

Enforcement Function

As part of its enforcement function, ATF agents investigate individuals and organizations that violate U.S. laws by illegally supplying guns to individuals prohibited from having them.[19] ATF refers criminal violations to United States Attorneys' Offices (USAO) or to state prosecutors for prosecution.

---

[17] ATF and other U.S. law enforcement agencies working in Mexico do not have authority to conduct investigations there, but they provide assistance and share information with Mexican agencies and their counterparts in the United States.

[18] All ATF personnel in Mexico are considered part of the Mexico Country Office, which is organizationally aligned under ATF's Office of International Affairs.

[19] Categories of prohibited individuals are defined in 18 U.S.C. § 922(g).

ATF tracks the status of investigations and refers investigative leads within ATF using its automated case management system, N-Force. Project Gunrunner cases were not initially identified in N-Force, but after 2006 ATF created a specific N-Force code for Project Gunrunner cases and directed its personnel to begin using it.

ATF considers any investigation conducted nationwide to be a "Project Gunrunner case" if it involves firearms trafficking or violent crime with a nexus to the Southwest border. This could include cases also coded as gang-related or as another type of case. Our discussion of Project Gunrunner cases in this report is based on ATF data that meets this definition.

Laws Governing Firearms Trafficking and Private Sales of Guns

There is no specific federal statute specifically prohibiting firearms trafficking. Consequently, when ATF agents identify trafficking operations and develop cases to refer to prosecutors, they use various federal and state charges. In addition, some existing federal regulations and statutes, such as those that require transaction records or background checks, do not apply to sales of guns between private individuals.[20]

Project Gunrunner Federal Statutes Used by ATF

ATF agents work with federal prosecutors to charge Project Gunrunner defendants under a wide range of federal statutes, not all of which directly cite firearms offenses, such as conspiracy charges and drug offenses. Between FY 2004 and FY 2009, ATF used 75 different statutes to seek federal prosecutions of Project Gunrunner defendants. These statutes prohibit activities associated with firearms trafficking – such as falsifying information when purchasing a gun and dealing guns without a license. Table 1 provides a list, in ascending order of statute number, of the 10 statutes most frequently used in ATF's Project Gunrunner referrals for prosecution during that period. We discuss ATF's referrals and USAOs' prosecutions of Project Gunrunner cases in Part III of this report.

---

[20] Some federal regulations and statutes do apply to the private sale of guns, such as the prohibition of transfers to known convicted felons. Additionally, some states have enacted laws regulating transfers of firearms between private individuals.

Table 1: Top 10 Statutes Used in Cases Referred for Prosecution of Project Gunrunner Defendants (FY 2004 through FY 2009)

Statute	Statute Definition
18 U.S.C. § (2)	Aiding and abetting
18 U.S.C. § 371	Conspiracy to commit offense against the United States*
18 U.S.C. § 922(a)(1)(A)	Willfully engage in firearms business without a license
18 U.S.C. § 922(a)(6)	Knowingly making a false statement in connection with a firearm purchase
18 U.S.C. § 922(g)(1)	Knowing possession of a firearm by a convicted felon
18 U.S.C. § 922(g)(5)	Knowing possession of a firearm by an illegal alien
18 U.S.C. § 924(a)(1)(A)	Knowingly making a false statement
18 U.S.C. § 924(c)	Use of a firearm in a federal drug or violent crime
21 U.S.C. § 841(a)(1)	Manufacturer, distribution, or possession of a controlled substance
21 U.S.C. § 846	Drug conspiracy

* 18 U.S.C. § 371 does not relate specifically to crimes involving firearms. Rather, according to Executive Office for United States Attorneys, prosecutors use the charge when there are no other conspiracy charges applicable to a case, often as part of the plea bargaining process.

Source: ATF data on federal statutes referred to USAOs for prosecution.

Private Sales of Guns

When an individual buys a gun from a licensed gun dealer, the purchaser must show proper identification to the gun dealer, fill out a federal Firearms Transaction Record (Form 4473), including personal information (such as name and address) and a short questionnaire to determine eligibility to purchase a gun, and submit to a National Instant Criminal Background Check System check.[21] The gun dealer retains a copy

---

[21] Mandated by the *Brady Handgun Violence Prevention Act of 1993* and launched by the FBI on November 30, 1998, the National Instant Criminal Background Check System is used by gun dealers to instantly determine whether a prospective buyer is eligible to possess guns or explosives. Before completing the sale, a gun dealer employee calls the FBI or another designated agency to ensure that the customer does not have a criminal record or is not otherwise ineligible to possess a gun because, for example, the buyer has been adjudicated as mentally defective. More than 100 million such checks have been made in the last decade, leading to more than 700,000 denials, according to the FBI (www.fbi.gov/hq/cjisd/nics.htm).

of the Form 4473 as a permanent record of the transfer of the weapon. This enables ATF to determine who originally purchased a gun if it is subsequently seized by law enforcement investigating a crime involving the gun.

Individuals who buy guns from an unlicensed private seller in a "secondary market venue" (such as gun shows, flea markets, and Internet sites) are exempt from the requirements of federal law to show identification, complete the Form 4473, and undergo a National Instant Criminal Background Check System check. Therefore, according to ATF and other Department officials we interviewed, individuals prohibited by law from possessing guns can easily obtain them from private sellers and do so without any federal records of the transactions. According to these officials, gun shows are a primary source of weapons for Mexican drug cartels. Generally, ATF can most readily trace a gun to the individual who first purchased it from a gun dealer. ATF has limited ability to trace used firearms sold by gun dealers and generally cannot trace privately sold guns to the private purchaser.

Regulatory Function

ATF regulates the firearms industry through licensing and inspections of gun dealers. The objective of ATF's application inspections is to ensure that only qualified individuals receive a license to sell guns. Also, ATF Industry Operations Investigators conduct periodic regulatory inspections of gun dealers by reviewing records, inventory, and the dealers' conduct of business. During these inspections, ATF educates gun dealers about trafficking indicators and how to report suspicious behaviors to ATF. Through these activities, ATF seeks to deter the diversion of guns from lawful commerce into the illegal market, where, among other uses, they may be trafficked to Mexico.

ATF tracks the status and results of its gun dealer inspections using its automated N-Spect system. ATF considers any inspection conducted in the Southwest border states – California, Arizona, New Mexico, and Texas – as Project Gunrunner-related. In Part I of this report, we describe the number of inspections conducted by ATF before and during Project Gunrunner.

Intelligence Function

ATF collects, analyzes, and disseminates firearms trafficking-related intelligence and has developed specialized information and intelligence resources to provide direction and focus to its enforcement and regulatory functions. Under Project Gunrunner, ATF seeks to provide agents with comprehensive information to detect, investigate, apprehend, and refer for prosecution individuals who illegally traffic guns. For example, ATF agents and intelligence personnel collect intelligence from gun dealers' reports on the sales of multiple handguns. Similarly, Industry Operations Investigators use intelligence-based risk factors as a part of their process for determining which gun dealers to inspect.

ATF's intelligence structure consists of both headquarters-level and field entities, as described below:

ATF Headquarters. ATF's Office of Strategic Intelligence and Information provides field personnel with intelligence to identify patterns and trends in firearms trafficking and related crime. In September 2008, this Office established a Field Intelligence Support Team dedicated to the Southwest border. Although ATF is not a recognized member of the national intelligence community, the Office of Strategic Intelligence and Information interacts with national and international intelligence agencies. Included in the Office's structure is ATF's Gun Desk at EPIC, which is a central repository for weapons-related intelligence. The Violent Crime Analysis Branch, co-located with ATF's National Tracing Center in Martinsburg, West Virginia, also falls under the Office of Strategic Intelligence and Information. Intelligence analysts at the Violent Crime Analysis Branch analyze and disseminate gun trace data and other intelligence to field personnel.

ATF Field Divisions. Each of ATF's 25 field divisions typically has a Field Intelligence Group, whose mission is to collect, evaluate, and disseminate tactical and strategic intelligence to the division's field offices.[22] Although the Office of Strategic Intelligence and Information provides strategic intelligence to all of ATF, each field division's Field Intelligence Group is considered the main intelligence asset for that division. Field Intelligence Groups receive information from a variety of ATF and external sources (Figure 3). Staffing varies, but Field Intelligence Groups generally include a supervisor (an agent), one to two Intelligence Officers (also agents), one to two Industry Operations Intelligence Specialists, two to four Intelligence Research Specialists, one to two Investigative Analysts, and one secretary.[23]

---

[22] ATF defines tactical intelligence as information produced to support operations or that relates to the specific time, date, nature, and other details of events. Strategic intelligence is defined as information required for the formulation of policy and plans at the regional, national, and international levels. Strategic intelligence differs primarily from tactical intelligence in level of use but may also vary in scope and detail.

[23] The *ATF Field Intelligence Group Supervisor's Guide Book* (September 2009) discusses the Field Intelligence Group composition and member responsibilities.

Figure 3: ATF Intelligence Sharing Process

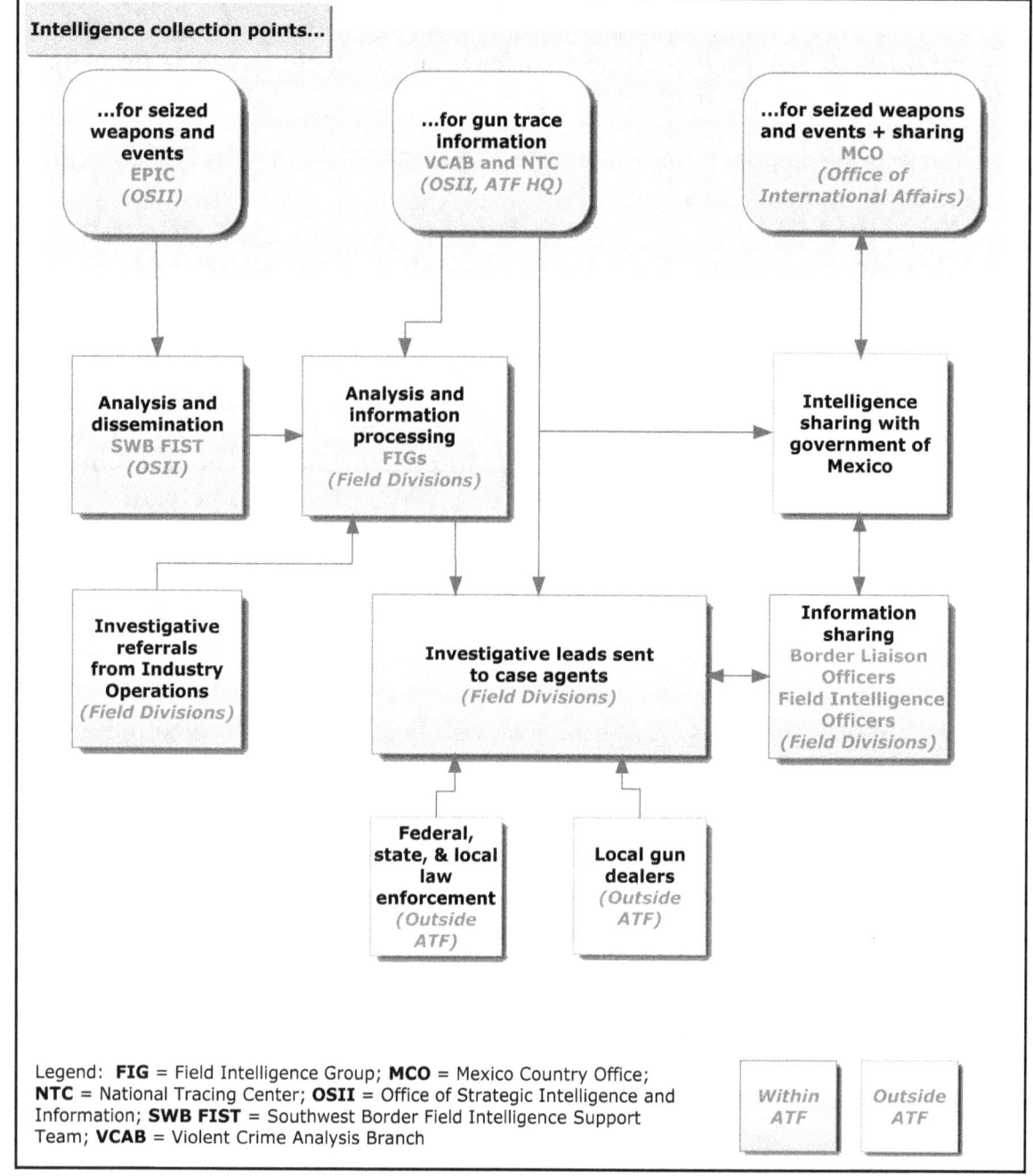

Note: The figure depicts a simplified version of ATF's general process.

Source: OIG.

Intelligence Collection Plan and ATF Intelligence Sharing Process. In 2009, the Office of Strategic Intelligence and Information distributed to all field divisions ATF's first Intelligence Collection Plan for Project Gunrunner. ATF published the plan intending that each field division would tailor it to its own operational needs. The plan stated that "ATF must develop a 'bee-hive mentality' whereby everyone works toward a common goal," identifying intelligence gaps and collecting information that ultimately results in intelligence products to be acted upon.[24] According to the plan, the Office of Strategic Intelligence and Information is to share with Mexican law enforcement "real-time, actionable intelligence relating to firearms trafficking networks" operating in the United States and Mexico. To accomplish this goal, ATF Field Intelligence Group supervisors, Resident Agents in Charge, and other field supervisors are to determine and prioritize intelligence requirements. The plan also focuses on the continuous collection and reporting of information to EPIC, which the plan states is responsible for directing the intelligence collection effort.

Additionally, the ATF Violent Crime Analysis Branch and the National Tracing Center disseminate gun trace data, information from reports on multiple sales of handguns, and other information to Field Intelligence Groups and field agents, who review the information to detect firearms trafficking patterns and to further their investigations. Industry Operations Investigators also make referrals to agents, through the Field Intelligence Group when they find potential evidence of firearms trafficking during gun dealer inspections. Local gun dealers and other law enforcement agencies provide intelligence directly to ATF agents, investigators, and the Field Intelligence Group.

Gun Tracing and eTrace

Gun tracing enables ATF to track a gun from its manufacturer or importer to a wholesaler and retail dealer, and then identify the gun's original retail purchaser. U.S. law does not require the tracking of private sales of guns, except for weapons subject to the *National Firearms Act.*[25]

---

[24] ATF, Project Gunrunner Southwest Border Initiative Intelligence Collection Plan, Update FY 2010 (November 2009), 4.

[25] The *National Firearms Act,* enacted in 1934, limits the availability of machine guns, short-barreled shotguns, short-barreled rifles, sound suppressors (silencers), and other similar weapons that were often used by criminals during the Prohibition Era. The *Gun Control Act of 1968* expanded the scope of the *National Firearms Act* to include destructive devices (for example, explosive and incendiary bombs, flash bang grenades, and weapons with a bore of greater than one-half inch in diameter), machine gun frames or receivers, and conversion kits for machine guns.

Tracing can help ATF identify trafficking corridors, patterns, schemes, traffickers, accomplices, and straw purchasers.[26]

To initiate a gun trace, the law enforcement agency that recovers a crime gun provides ATF's National Tracing Center with the gun's serial number and other information required to identify it to the exclusion of all other firearms. The National Tracing Center responds with the gun's purchase history and other information. Law enforcement agencies may submit a trace by facsimile, telephone, or through ATF's Internet-based eTrace system.

The eTrace system can be accessed directly by ATF personnel and other law enforcement agencies worldwide. It allows law enforcement agencies to submit gun trace requests electronically, to monitor the progress of the traces electronically, and to retrieve completed results of their own agency's trace requests. Using eTrace, authorized law enforcement representatives can also access a historical database of their agency's own trace-related data and generate analytical reports and investigative lead information. The representatives of one agency cannot access the results of other agencies' trace requests at this time. However, according to ATF, system modifications are in development to allow agencies to share trace data with each other in accordance with, and subject to, new appropriations laws.

To provide Mexican law enforcement authorities with direct access to gun tracing, ATF developed eTrace 4.0, also known as Spanish eTrace, which receives and provides trace results in Spanish. In December 2009, ATF piloted a program to deploy Spanish eTrace to, and to train Mexican officials in, the system's use. Initially, ATF planned to provide Spanish eTrace to all federal and state police laboratories in Mexico. However, as of June 2010, ATF staff told us that Mexican state laboratories were not able to use Spanish eTrace because of objections from the Mexican federal government (discussed further in this report).[27] The eTrace system is the primary source of investigative leads pertaining to guns trafficked to Mexico.

---

[26] According to ATF, a "straw purchase" occurs when the actual buyer of a firearm uses another person, "the straw purchaser," to execute the paperwork necessary to purchase a firearm from a gun dealer. The actual buyer is often prohibited from purchasing the gun. The straw purchaser violates federal law by making a false statement with respect to the information required to be kept in the gun dealer's records. According to ATF, straw purchasing is one of the most frequent methods used to illegally acquire guns.

[27] In September 2010, ATF told us that it had deployed Spanish eTrace to all Spanish-language eTrace users in March 2010, including to Mexican federal law

Cont.

Organized Crime Drug Enforcement Task Force (OCDETF)

OCDETF is a Department of Justice program that seeks to combine resources and expertise of federal, state, and local law enforcement agencies to identify, disrupt, and dismantle organizations responsible for drug trafficking.[28] According to the OCDETF website, OCDETF targets not only the drug operations, but also the "tools of the trade" for these organizations, including money laundering and firearms trafficking.

When a case has been designated as an OCDETF case, the costs of the investigation – including travel, wiretaps, confidential informant subsistence, and other evidence-gathering expenses – may be reimbursed by the OCDETF Program, depending on funding availability. To have a case approved as an OCDETF case, an agency presents it to other agencies involved in the program, including the USAO with jurisdiction in the area. Once the case is vetted by a federal prosecutor designated to support the OCDETF Program, it is presented to one of nine regional OCDETF committees, which must give final approval before the program's resources are dedicated to the case.

The OCDETF Program also establishes task forces (which it refers to as strike forces) to permanently co-locate representatives from federal law enforcement agencies, along with representatives of state and local law enforcement, in a city. The participating agencies, including ATF when it chooses to do so, work together to investigate trafficking organizations. OCDETF task forces are currently located in San Diego, Phoenix, El Paso, Houston (including satellite offices in Laredo and McAllen), Tampa, San Juan, Atlanta, New York, and Boston. ATF's use of the OCDETF Program is discussed in Part III of this report.

ATF's Coordination with Other Federal Law Enforcement Agencies

To effectively implement Project Gunrunner, ATF must coordinate with other federal agencies within and outside of the Department of Justice

---

enforcement. Yet, as noted above, in June 2010, we were informed that Mexican laboratories were not using Spanish e-trace. As a result of a September 2010 eTrace memorandum of understanding between ATF and the government of Mexico, ATF plans to begin redeployment of Spanish eTrace in Mexico in November 2010 and to offer training to Mexican personnel in all 31 states.

[28] Agencies represented in the OCDETF Program include ATF, the DEA, the FBI, Immigration and Customs Enforcement, the U.S. Marshals Service, the Internal Revenue Service, and the U.S. Coast Guard – in cooperation with the Department of Justice Criminal Division, the Tax Division, and the 94 USAOs, as well as with state and local law enforcement.

---

that are involved in monitoring and protecting the U.S. border with Mexico. As discussed below, some of those agencies have their own programs that target firearms trafficking, either directly or indirectly.

Drug Enforcement Administration (DEA)

The DEA enforces controlled substance laws and regulations, and investigates organizations and individuals involved in the growing, manufacture, or distribution of controlled substances intended to be trafficked into the United States. Although DEA is primarily focused on drug trafficking enterprises, there is often a nexus between Mexican drug and firearms trafficking organizations. As a result, ATF and the DEA work together on various task forces in Southwest border locations and in Mexico.

United States Attorneys' Offices (USAO)

The USAOs determine which federal cases to prosecute within their jurisdictions. Each USAO is led by a presidentially appointed United States Attorney, who serves as the chief federal law enforcement officer for the judicial district. Under Project Gunrunner, ATF agents work directly with Assistant U.S. Attorneys (AUSA) to develop firearms trafficking-related cases for prosecution.

Department of State

The Department of State, through its Bureau for International Narcotics and Law Enforcement Affairs, provides training, operations, intelligence, and logistical support for foreign counternarcotics programs established by the U.S. *Foreign Assistance Act*.[29] In the U.S. Embassy in Mexico City, a Department of State Narcotics Affairs Section provides counternarcotics policy and strategy guidance to Ambassadors and facilitates funding and other support for the government of Mexico. Under Project Gunrunner, ATF works with staff from the Narcotic Affairs Section to provide Mexican officials with equipment and training on gun tracing and identification, and investigations.

Department of Homeland Security (DHS)

Immigration and Customs Enforcement (ICE). ICE, the largest investigative arm within DHS, investigates a wide range of domestic and international activities related to the illegal movement of people and goods

---

[29] 22 U.S.C. § 2151 et seq.

into, within, and out of the United States. ICE's investigative responsibilities include narcotics, weapons, and human smuggling, and export enforcement issues.

ATF's Project Gunrunner and ICE's Operation Armas Cruzadas both target firearms trafficking to Mexico, but the two initiatives target different points in the gun smuggling process. Launched in 2008 by ICE, Operation Armas Cruzadas is focused on trans-border weapons smuggling networks along the Southwest border. Project Gunrunner targets the trafficking of guns from the United States to Mexico through investigations of firearms found to have been trafficked into Mexico and related violent crime.

In addition, ATF and ICE have worked together on investigations involving firearms trafficking to Mexico through ATF's participation in several ICE-led, multi-agency Border Enforcement Security Task Forces.

Customs and Border Protection (CBP). The CBP inspects traffic entering the United States and, to a much lesser extent, traffic leaving the United States. The CBP seizes drugs, cash, guns, and other contraband as it is smuggled across the U.S. border. In Southwest border locations, ATF coordinates with the CBP regarding inspections of suspected firearms traffickers crossing the border.

ATF's Coordination with Mexican Agencies

Attorney General of the Republic – *Procuraduría General de la República* (PGR)

In Mexico, the Attorney General's office investigates and prosecutes Mexican federal crimes, including all gun-related offenses. Its staff includes investigators and intelligence analysts. ATF works with the Mexico Attorney General's office to obtain information used in gun tracing and for firearms trafficking investigations.

National Center for Information, Analysis, and Planning in Order to Fight Crime – *El Centro Nacional de Planeación, Análisis, e Información para el Combate a la Delincuencia* (CENAPI)

CENAPI, a unit of the Attorney General's office, contains analysts who conduct information gathering, intelligence analysis, and data dissemination. CENAPI researches areas of organized crime, including the largest organized crime threat in Mexico, drug cartels, and builds databases containing this intelligence. ATF works with CENAPI because it is the primary Mexican agency responsible for deploying Spanish eTrace (discussed later in this report) and for entering Mexican crime gun data into that system.

Secretariat of Public Security – *Secretaría de Seguridad Pública*

The Secretariat of Public Security is the Mexican law enforcement agency that has the authority to police and conduct investigations at a national level. According to U.S. law enforcement officials, the Secretariat of Public Security is being restructured and trained to better combat Mexican drug cartels and to form a force of "street cops" similar to its federal counterparts in the United States. ATF and other U.S. law enforcement agencies assist in the training of new officers and work with them on investigations.

Secretary of National Defense/Mexican Military – *La Secretaría de la Defensa Nacional*

The military in Mexico often supplements the efforts of law enforcement entities, giving it an important role in the conflict with the drug cartels and associated firearms trafficking activity. In areas of Mexico with particularly high levels of violent crime, the military has been assigned a public safety and policing role. The Mexican military is responsible for taking possession of and safeguarding guns and explosives seized in Mexico within a few days of being seized.

PURPOSE, SCOPE, AND METHODOLOGY OF THE OIG REVIEW

Purpose

This review examined ATF's implementation of Project Gunrunner's mission to reduce firearms trafficking to Mexico and related violent crime.[30] We examined ATF's execution of its enforcement and regulatory programs related to the Southwest border and Mexico, its effectiveness in developing and sharing intelligence, its traces of Mexican crime guns, its coordination with U.S. and Mexican law enforcement, and how ATF worked with USAOs to prosecute firearms traffickers.

Scope

We conducted our fieldwork from November 2009 through June 2010. We also gathered updated information from ATF through September 2010. In evaluating the impact of Project Gunrunner, we generally examined ATF activities from FY 2006, when the project became a national program, through FY 2009. When it was available, we also examined data from FY 2004 through FY 2009 to compare ATF's operations for 3 years before and after its implementation of Project Gunrunner.

This review is the second conducted by the Office of the Inspector General (OIG) on Project Gunrunner since 2009. The first review examined ATF's planning, hiring, staffing, and allocation of resources for Project Gunrunner, including its expenditure of $10 million in Recovery Act funds.[31] This second Project Gunrunner review continued the examination of ATF's procedures for coordinating among its Southwest border field divisions.

Methodology

In this review we conducted interviews; performance, trace, prosecutorial, and investigative data analyses; and document reviews. We also visited ATF's National Tracing Center and Violent Crime Analysis

---

[30] Although our review included ATF's efforts to reduce violent crime associated with firearms trafficking to Mexico, the causes of changes in the levels of violence along the border are numerous and are not attributable only to ATF's implementation of Project Gunrunner.

[31] U.S. Department of Justice Office of the Inspector General, *Interim Review of ATF's Project Gunrunner,* Evaluation and Inspections Report I-2009-006 (September 2009).

Branch in Martinsburg, West Virginia; ATF's Dallas, Phoenix, and Los Angeles Field Divisions; and its Mexico Country Office in Mexico City.[32]

Interviews

We conducted 99 in-person and telephone interviews with personnel from ATF headquarters, ATF's Dallas, Phoenix, and Los Angeles Field Divisions and selected offices, and the Mexico Country Office; the Executive Office for United States Attorneys (EOUSA) and USAOs in several Southwest border districts; the Department's Criminal Division; the DEA; the U.S. Department of State; DHS, including its ICE and CBP components; and military and law enforcement officials of the Mexican government. Appendix III provides a list of all interviewees.

Data Analysis

We analyzed several types of ATF and USAO data that generally covered FY 2004 through FY 2009. The ATF data included gun trace results from the Southwest border and Mexico, Project Gunrunner cases initiated and referred to USAOs for federal prosecution, inspections of gun dealers in the Southwest border states, and statistics on active gun dealers and multiple sales of handguns. We also reviewed data from ATF's case management system on Industry Operations Investigators' generation and referral of investigative leads to ATF agents. Finally, we analyzed USAO data from its Legal Information Office Network System (LIONS), on declinations of ATF's Project Gunrunner cases and of ATF-led joint cases that were referred to USAOs for prosecution. LIONS collects case information for federal criminal offenses, but does not track its cases as being Project Gunrunner cases.

Document Review

We reviewed ATF policies, guidelines, and plans relating to Project Gunrunner and firearms trafficking. These included operating plans, intelligence products, performance measures, directives and guidance to field personnel, and field office documents. We also reviewed ATF and EOUSA budget requests and resource justifications related to firearms trafficking and Southwest border operations. In addition, we reviewed EOUSA policies and guidelines related to the prosecution of ATF's firearms trafficking-related Project Gunrunner cases. We reviewed ATF managers'

---

[32] During the fieldwork for our previous report on Project Gunrunner, we also visited ATF's Houston Field Division and its McAllen Field Office, as well as the Las Cruces Field Office of the Phoenix Field Division. Some of the information we obtained from those interviews contributed to our findings in this report.

testimony and statements to Congress, as well as congressional testimony by EOUSA, DHS, and Office of the Attorney General officials on firearms trafficking and Southwest border violence.

Consistent with our standard practice, on September 3, 2010, we provided a working draft of this report to ATF and other components and agencies for their review and comment. In response to their comments, as well as a result of updated data and information provided by ATF, we made some changes to the working draft where appropriate.

PART I: ATF'S EXPANDED EFFORTS IN SUPPORT OF PROJECT GUNRUNNER

Through Project Gunrunner, ATF has increased several of its program activities related to firearms trafficking, including the number of gun trace submissions, the number of investigations it initiated, the number of these investigations it subsequently referred for prosecution, and the number of defendants it referred for prosecution. ATF also increased the number of compliance inspections it conducted, the hours spent by its Southwest border field divisions on inspections, and the number of referrals Industry Operations made to Criminal Enforcement for investigation.

ATF's approach to combating firearms trafficking and related violence along the Southwest border, as articulated in its June 2007 Gunrunner strategy, has been to focus on key activities, including tracing guns to identify traffickers and patterns, conducting criminal investigations of traffickers, conducting compliance inspections of gun dealers in the region, and referring leads from Industry Operations to Criminal Enforcement. Relevant activities are tracked in ATF's case management (N-Force) and inspections (N-Spect) databases, and its tracing system (eTrace).

In the section below, we describe our analysis of seven categories of data from these databases to measure Project Gunrunner's performance:

- gun trace requests received from U.S. and Mexican locations,
- Project Gunrunner cases initiated,
- cases referred for prosecution,
- defendants referred for prosecution,
- completed gun dealer compliance inspections,
- hours spent on gun dealer compliance inspections, and
- referrals from Industry Operations to Criminal Enforcement.[33]

As stated in the Background section of this report, ATF considers any investigation conducted nationwide to be a Project Gunrunner case if it involves firearms trafficking or violent crime with a nexus to the Southwest

---

[33] ATF's strategic plan for FY 2010 to FY 2016 included broad performance measures of firearms trafficking. Three of the performance measures were similar to those we analyzed: number of defendants referred for prosecution for violation of firearms trafficking laws, number of firearms trafficking investigations initiated, and number of traces submitted.

border. Throughout this report, any reference made to a Project Gunrunner case, to referrals of cases, or to referrals of defendants for prosecution uses ATF's definition.

For measures relating to trace submissions and Industry Operations inspections, we compared the 3-year period before ATF's implementation of Project Gunrunner (FY 2004 through FY 2006) with the 3-year period after ATF's initiation of Project Gunrunner (FY 2007 through FY 2009). For measures relating to Project Gunrunner cases, we examined only the period after the initiative began (FY 2007 through FY 2009).[34]

We found that since implementing Project Gunrunner, ATF has increased its gun trace submissions from U.S. Southwest border locations and from Mexico, the number of investigations ATF initiated, the number of cases ATF subsequently referred for prosecution, and the number of defendants ATF referred for prosecution. ATF also increased the number of compliance inspections conducted in its Southwest border field divisions and the number of referrals Industry Operations made to Criminal Enforcement for investigation. These trends are depicted in Figure 4 (below) and discussed further below. We also found that ATF increased its efforts under Project Gunrunner through its Gun Runner Impact Team initiative, a targeted 120-day effort implemented in the Houston Field Division during summer 2009.

The number of traces of U.S. and Mexican crime guns has increased since Project Gunrunner began.

ATF's June 2007 Gunrunner strategy describes tracing as an essential tool for identifying potential traffickers and the "cornerstone" of Project Gunrunner. We found that ATF has increased tracing along the Southwest border and in Mexico. From FY 2004 through FY 2006, the four Southwest border field divisions and Mexico traced, on average, 20 percent of all traces requested from the United States and Mexico (143,024 of 714,472 traces).[35] The number of such traces increased to 26 percent (207,609 of 804,136 traces) in FY 2007 through FY 2009.

---

[34] Although ATF initiated cases involving firearms trafficking and related violent crime prior to FY 2007, our attempt to analyze the 3-year period prior to ATF's initiation of Project Gunrunner did not generate reliable results. ATF had not developed a program code to track these cases until after the initiative began in 2006, and ATF was unable to fully identify firearms trafficking and other cases from FY 2004 through FY 2006 that would be comparable to Project Gunrunner cases. Therefore, a comparison of firearms trafficking cases prior to FY 2007 would result in an overstatement of the increase in firearms trafficking cases that resulted from Project Gunrunner.

[35] Different ATF offices analyze trace data in different ways. The National Tracing Center typically reports annual trace numbers according to the date the trace was submitted. In comparison, the Violent Crime Analysis Branch bases its analyses on the

Cont.

The largest percentage increase in traces during Project Gunrunner occurred in traces from Mexico. From FY 2004 through FY 2006, traces of Mexican crime guns accounted for only 1 percent of all traces (9,256 traces). Since the start of Project Gunrunner, in FY 2007 through FY 2009, Mexican traces increased to 8 percent of all traces (62,606 traces). The increase in traces of Mexican crime guns from FY 2004 through 2006 to FY 2007 through 2009 was 576 percent.

---

date a gun was recovered, but if no recovery date exists, it will use the trace date. This results in differences between the annual trace number reported by the National Tracing Center and the Violent Crime Analysis Branch because there are typically delays between when Mexican crime guns are recovered and when they are submitted for tracing. In this report, we base our analysis on data provided by the Violent Crime Analysis Branch.

Figure 4: ATF Project Gunrunner Performance Measures

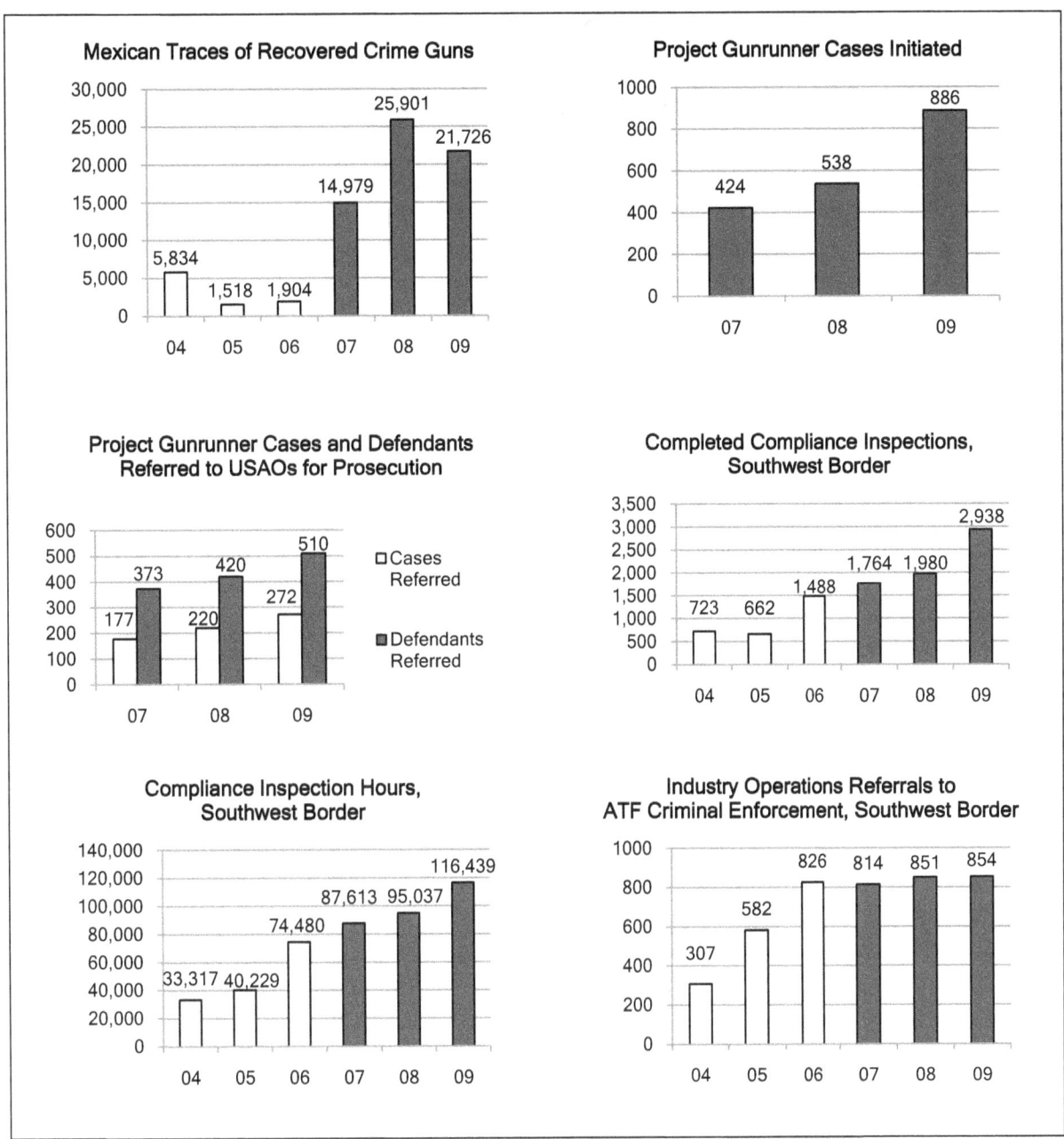

Note: Yellow indicates results before Project Gunrunner's inception (FY 2004 through FY 2006), and blue indicates results since the project was implemented (FY 2007 through FY 2009).

Sources: OIG analysis of ATF Violent Crime Analysis Branch and Office of Strategic Management data.

Cases initiated, referred for prosecution, and defendants referred for prosecution for firearms trafficking to Mexico or related violent crime also increased during Project Gunrunner.

We also determined that ATF significantly increased the number of cases involving firearms trafficking or violent crime with a nexus to the Southwest border that it initiated after the implementation of Project Gunrunner in 2006. ATF initiated 424 such cases in FY 2007, 538 in FY 2008, and 886 in FY 2009, an increase of 109 percent in that period.[36]

The number of cases involving firearms trafficking or violent crime with a nexus to the Southwest border that ATF referred to USAOs for prosecution also increased after Project Gunrunner began. ATF referred 177 such cases for prosecution in FY 2007, 220 in FY 2008, and 272 in FY 2009, an increase of 54 percent.

The number of defendants referred to USAOs for prosecution for firearms trafficking or violent crime with a nexus to the Southwest border also increased since the start of Project Gunrunner. ATF referred 373 defendants for prosecution in FY 2007, 420 in FY 2008, and 510 in FY 2009, an increase of 37 percent.

The numbers of gun dealer compliance inspections conducted, inspection hours, and inspection referrals to Criminal Enforcement increased during Project Gunrunner.

Since Project Gunrunner began, ATF has increased the number of both gun dealer compliance inspections and the compliance inspection hours worked by the Southwest border field divisions. From FY 2004 through FY 2006, ATF completed 2,873 compliance inspections in the region. During that period, ATF personnel worked a total of 148,026 hours on compliance inspections there. The number of compliance inspections increased 133 percent after Project Gunrunner began to 6,682 between FY 2007 and FY 2009. The number of compliance inspection hours worked also increased to 299,089 between FY 2007 and FY 2009, an increase of 102 percent.

Since FY 2004, the four ATF Southwest border field divisions have increased the number of Industry Operations referrals to law enforcement, which includes referrals handled within ATF and those sent to other federal,

---

[36] Although the data that ATF provided to the OIG showed that the number of Project Gunrunner cases initiated by ATF increased from FY 2007 through FY 2009, the total number of cases specifically related to firearms initiated by ATF nationwide decreased by 909 cases (5 percent) in the same time period, from 17,548 in FY 2007 to 16,639 in FY 2009.

state, and local law enforcement agencies. Industry Operations referrals are typically created during or after a gun dealer inspection. There are no minimum guidelines as to what triggers a referral, but Industry Operations Investigators are trained to identify potential illegal activity.

To determine the number of referrals ATF made and their outcomes we analyzed all the inspection referrals to ATF Criminal Enforcement personnel contained in the data provided by ATF. Industry Operations staff made 1,715 referrals to ATF Criminal Enforcement from FY 2004 through FY 2006 in the four Southwest border field divisions. The number of such referrals increased 47 percent after Project Gunrunner began, to 2,519 from FY 2007 through FY 2009.[37]

ATF used its temporary Gun Runner Impact Team initiative to increase inspections and case initiations in the Houston Field Division.

ATF also increased its efforts under Project Gunrunner through its Gun Runner Impact Team initiative, a temporary deployment of 100 agents, Industry Operations Investigators, and support staff to the Houston Field Division during summer 2009. ATF deployed the personnel for 120 days to address a backlog in investigative leads and gun dealer inspections in the Houston Field Division and "aggressively target and disrupt groups and organizations responsible for trafficking firearms to Mexico."[38]

According to an October 2009 Department press release, the initiative involved investigating over 1,100 investigative leads, which resulted in opening 276 firearms trafficking cases involving the seizure of over 440 illegal firearms and other contraband. In an internal assessment of the initiative's outcome, ATF stated that several of these cases related directly to Mexican drug cartels and involved one or more individuals who had recruited several straw purchasers who purchased firearms that were then trafficked to Mexico. On the regulatory side, ATF reported that Industry Operations conducted over 1,000 gun dealer inspections, which led to 440 violations. In September 2010, ATF announced the conclusion of another Gun Runner Impact Team initiative in the Phoenix Field Division, reporting that the Phoenix team had initiated 174 firearms trafficking cases, seized 1,300 illegally trafficked firearms, and conducted over 800 gun dealer inspections.

---

[37] ATF Industry Operations staff also made 791 referrals to state and local law enforcement agencies and to other federal agencies such as ICE, the FBI, and the Internal Revenue Service.

[38] Department of Justice press release, Justice Department Announces Success in Battle Against Firearms Trafficking and Recovery Act Funds to Build on Project Gunrunner (October 1, 2009).

PART II: ATF FIREARMS TRAFFICKING INTELLIGENCE AND INFORMATION

> **Under Project Gunrunner, ATF does not systematically share strategic intelligence with its Mexican and U.S. partner agencies, and ATF Southwest border Field Intelligence Groups are not consistently providing actionable investigative leads to field agents. ATF also needs to better implement its Border Liaison Program to improve information sharing and coordination between ATF's U.S. and Mexico elements.**

ATF and its Mexican and U.S. partner agencies are not systematically and consistently sharing strategic intelligence needed to combat firearms trafficking to Mexico.

ATF's partnerships with other U.S. agencies and the Mexican government are a critical component of Project Gunrunner. ATF's Project Gunrunner strategy states that each ATF intelligence entity "must be diligent in its exercise of information flow to and from . . . other domestic and Mexican counterparts."[39]

However, we found that strategic intelligence on drug cartel firearms trafficking activity – including trends and patterns in their operations, the locations where they are operating, and the composition of their membership and associates – is not consistently shared between ATF and Mexican law enforcement, and between ATF, the CBP, DEA, and ICE. Although ATF has shared some strategic intelligence products with these agencies, it is not doing so systematically and regularly.[40]

Mexican law enforcement reports that ATF's exchange of strategic intelligence is incomplete.

Although the government of Mexico has intensified its national efforts to counter the drug cartels, Mexican officials told us they have sought but not received strategic intelligence from ATF on patterns and trends of

---

[39] ATF, *Southwest Border Initiative: Project Gunrunner* (June 2007), 16.

[40] ATF has identified the need to improve intelligence sharing with Mexican and U.S. law enforcement partners and improve its understanding of intelligence gaps in a recent strategy document entitled "Project Gunrunner – A Cartel Focused Strategy" (September 2010, cartel strategy). In that document, ATF stated that its efforts to combat firearms trafficking "will require greater collaboration between ATF field divisions and other law enforcement and intelligence agencies."

firearms trafficking from the United States to Mexico. For example, in a November 2009 monthly U.S.-Mexico GC Armas meeting on firearms trafficking, Mexican officials asked ATF for additional information and intelligence concerning the routes, destinations, and Mexican nationals that might be involved in firearms trafficking activity.[41]

Mexican officials reiterated the need for strategic intelligence on firearms trafficking during our interviews with them in March 2010. Senior Mexican law enforcement officials from the Mexico Attorney General's office (PGR) and from that office's intelligence unit (CENAPI) told us that it is important to their efforts to have more intelligence on how guns are being trafficked from the United States into Mexico. Mexican military representatives also said they could achieve better results interdicting guns if they had more intelligence on where and how guns are crossing the U.S. border into Mexico, including the routes used to traffic higher-caliber weapons into Mexico. As described below, we found that ATF has already developed intelligence products on these and other topics of interest to Mexican officials.[42]

Further, PGR officials stated that PGR develops its own intelligence about firearms trafficking and Mexican drug cartels, but ATF has not requested it from PGR, and the two agencies have not shared such information. Mexican law enforcement officials told us that if there were more coordination with ATF in developing such intelligence, they would be able to help identify firearms trafficking trends and patterns on the U.S. side of the border to assist ATF in its domestic mission.

Our review found that some of the information sought by Mexican officials has already been identified as strategic intelligence that ATF can share with the government of Mexico. For example, ATF's November 2009 Intelligence Collection Plan includes a list of the existing "actionable intelligence products" that ATF can share with Mexican law enforcement. We found that many of these items are the same strategic intelligence products that Mexican officials have requested but reported that they are

---

[41] GC Armas is a monthly meeting held at CENAPI headquarters in Mexico City that serves as the coordinating entity for joint U.S.-Mexico operations related to the detection, monitoring, and detention of arms trafficking suspects crossing the border. U.S. agencies that attend GC Armas are ATF, ICE, the DEA, Defense Attaché Office (Department of Defense), FBI, CBP, Narcotics Affairs Section, and Office of Foreign Assets Control (Department of the Treasury). Mexican law enforcement agencies in attendance are the PGR and the PGR's CENAPI, the Mexican Foreign Ministry, Mexican Military, Mexican Navy, the Secretariat of Public Security, Customs, and the National Security and Investigation Center (intelligence agency).

[42] We reviewed other Office of Strategic Intelligence and Information products, including maps illustrating firearms trafficking corridors, analyses of gun source locations, and drug cartels' weapons of choice.

not receiving, such as firearms trafficking routes, safe house locations, distribution points and destinations, lists of weapons and ammunition being trafficked, and other documents related to firearms trafficking.

We asked ATF officials about the sharing of this type of information with Mexico. ATF responded that its Mexico Country Office has provided Mexican officials with strategic intelligence on firearms trafficking and has repeatedly presented the requested intelligence at various venues with Mexican officials, including at the GC Armas meetings, through EPIC, and through border liaison personnel detailed to the Office of Strategic Intelligence and Information. According to ATF, however, there have been internal coordination problems between government of Mexico agencies, which we also found through our fieldwork.

We determined that much of the intelligence ATF cited as having exchanged with Mexican officials is tactical or investigative in nature, rather than strategic intelligence. Moreover, some of the exchanges occur informally, which reduces the utility and availability of the intelligence to ATF's Mexican counterparts. For example, ATF cited a border liaison who provided strategic and tactical intelligence informally to Mexican counterparts at a local working group. While ATF's informal information exchanges with Mexican officials are intended to improve its working relationship with the government of Mexico and contribute to investigations on both sides of the border, this process has not resulted in intended recipients in each Mexican agency receiving important strategic intelligence or ATF receiving strategic intelligence from Mexican agencies.

ATF's exchange of strategic intelligence with the DEA and ICE is inconsistent and lacking in some instances.

ATF's Gunrunner strategy states that ATF should work with the DEA and ICE to shut down firearms trafficking operations. We found that ATF does not consistently share strategic intelligence about firearms trafficking with the DEA and ICE. Consequently, ATF and these agencies may be targeting the same groups and individuals in an uncoordinated manner.

Project Gunrunner cases target many of the same cartel organizations that DEA and ICE enforcement operations target. Gaps and failures in the exchange of intelligence among these agencies create the potential for duplication of effort, inefficiency, and the risk of operational compromise. A 2008 internal intelligence assessment of Project Gunrunner acknowledged that ATF's information about Mexican cartels was "haphazard."[43] The assessment continued by stating that with more communication and

---

[43] ATF, 2008 Project Gunrunner Assessment, November 19, 2009.

collaboration with other federal law enforcement agencies, "this intelligence gap will shrink."

However, ATF's Office of Strategic Intelligence and Information has not established a method to systematically share strategic intelligence with the DEA. The Office established intelligence liaisons at several federal agencies, including at the DEA, but the liaisons at the DEA are not assigned there for the purpose of exchanging strategic intelligence related to firearms trafficking. Rather, the ATF Chief of the Office's Criminal Intelligence Division confirmed that the duties of the ATF's liaisons assigned to the DEA are related to the Department's international organized crime mission, not Project Gunrunner or the Southwest border. The ATF Chief told the OIG that it would be helpful if his agency had intelligence from the DEA on the cartels, especially identified cartel members and weapons they might possess.

DEA officials told us they have compiled a large amount of intelligence on the drug cartels and that the exchange of this intelligence with ATF would be of great strategic value. However, an official of the DEA's Mexico and Central America office, an office that targets drug cartels' narcotics operations and complements Project Gunrunner, was unaware of the existence of a strategic intelligence counterpart organization at ATF's Office of Strategic Intelligence and Information. Consequently, the DEA did not know with whom to coordinate and share information at ATF. The Chief of Strategic Intelligence added that the DEA needs a counterpart at ATF because "weapons are a necessary tool of drug traffickers in waging their wars and battles."

ICE officials stated that they would benefit from having ATF strategic intelligence, such as time-to-crime patterns, types of guns seized in Mexico, and methods used by traffickers to obtain guns from gun shows or through straw purchasers at gun dealers. One ICE Special Agent in Charge told us that this type of intelligence would help ICE better orient its efforts on smuggling investigations. ICE agents also said they would be able to use any intelligence ATF offered on trafficking organizations and their practices in ICE's efforts to build complex conspiracy cases against firearm traffickers. ICE officials told us that in exchange, they could provide ATF with strategic intelligence developed on firearms trafficking to Mexico and on Mexican drug cartels and their activities.

Officials from ATF's Criminal Intelligence Division told us that the lack of an exchange of strategic intelligence not only hinders ATF's effectiveness at gaining valuable intelligence on Project Gunrunner targets, but also inhibits ICE's ability to conduct its closely related firearm interdiction missions.

We asked ATF officials why this strategic intelligence was not being shared with DEA and ICE officials and why they had not requested such intelligence from the DEA and ICE. ATF responded that it has shared strategic intelligence products on firearms trafficking with other U.S. law enforcement agencies, including the DEA and ICE. However, ATF's strategic intelligence counterparts in both the DEA and ICE reported to us that they have not received this information. As with Mexican law enforcement officials, we believe that the strategic intelligence sharing process should be more systematic and that established counterparts in ATF, the DEA, and ICE should be identified to facilitate the two-way exchange of information in a timely manner.

ATF shares some tactical intelligence with the DEA and CBP in support of their respective trafficking investigations, but the benefits have been limited.

We found that ATF shares some tactical intelligence and coordinates well with the DEA and CBP in their field operations, but the frequency and effectiveness of the coordination varies by location. Coordination between ATF and the CBP has not resulted in significant numbers of seizures of guns going into Mexico.

At locations across the Southwest border, ATF and DEA personnel both reported to us that when the DEA has a lead that pertains to firearms violations or trafficking, it passes the lead to ATF. For example, in McAllen, Texas, one ATF supervisor reported that his office receives so many leads resulting from DEA seizures that it has put a strain on ATF resources in that city. An ATF Special Agent in Charge of a Southwest border field division also told the OIG that even though the DEA has not traditionally done so there, it is beginning to provide ATF with tips related to firearms trafficking that its personnel hear from wiretaps and other intelligence sources. ATF had not provided as much of this intelligence to the DEA, although DEA field staff we interviewed said they were content with the level of support they were receiving from ATF, especially with ATF's expertise in guns.

An ATF Southwest border Special Agent in Charge told us he considers CBP staff to be counterparts with whom ATF works well on a shared mission. ATF intelligence staff in the field and at EPIC also post "lookouts" into the CBP's database, which the CBP then uses to identify vehicles or individuals to search during southbound inspections. When CBP personnel seize weapons, they either notify ATF or ICE.[44]

---

[44] See Part VI of this report for additional information on CBP and ATF coordination on operations at the border.

Despite the cooperation, CBP has not seized significant numbers of guns going into Mexico. According to a Government Accountability Office (GAO) report on firearms trafficking, although the CBP has increased its southbound inspections of vehicles to interdict contraband such as guns going into Mexico, the CBP has been unable to seize many weapons. In FY 2008, there were only 70 weapons interdicted as a part of southbound inspections.[45] Similarly, an internal DHS report found that in the 9-month period spanning March 24 to December 28, 2009, the CBP seized only 93 weapons being transported to Mexico through points of entry along the Southwest border. CBP officials we interviewed told us that gun seizures are typically the result of the CBP's incidental inspections – such as random vehicle searches conducted because of officers' instincts, canine usage, or targeted southbound inspections – rather than intelligence provided by ATF.

CBP officials said that any information ATF collects on the activities of traffickers to transport guns across the border into Mexico could benefit the CBP's implementation of its southbound inspection program. With more detailed intelligence from ATF on individuals, vehicles, or a large purchase of guns, the CBP could focus its enforcement operations at specific, relevant points along the border and interdict guns and other contraband being trafficked to Mexico.

Is sum, it is crucial that ATF maintain close partnerships with other U.S. agencies and the government of Mexico to combat the flow of firearms to Mexican drug cartels. Although ATF has shared strategic intelligence products with Mexican and other U.S. agencies, it is not doing so consistently and systematically. For example, we found that ATF is not systematically sharing strategic intelligence on cartel firearms trafficking – including trends and patterns in their operations, where they are operating, and the composition of their membership and associates – with Mexican law enforcement, the DEA, or ICE. While ATF regularly shares tactical intelligence on firearms trafficking suspects and activities with the DEA and CBP, the benefits to CBP have been limited. We believe ATF could better combat firearms trafficking if it improved its sharing of strategic intelligence with its partner agencies.

---

[45] U.S. Government Accountability Office, *Firearms Trafficking: U.S. Efforts to Combat Arms Trafficking to Mexico Face Planning and Coordination Challenges,* GAO-09-709 (June 2009).

Recommendation

We recommend that ATF:

1. Coordinate with the government of Mexico, the CBP, DEA, and ICE to ensure systematic and regular exchanges of strategic intelligence to combat firearms trafficking to Mexico.

ATF Southwest border Field Intelligence Groups are not consistently providing actionable investigative leads to field agents.

As discussed below, ATF personnel along the Southwest border told us that agents investigating Project Gunrunner cases are not consistently receiving timely, actionable intelligence from ATF's Field Intelligence Groups.[46]

Agents investigating Project Gunrunner cases say they are not receiving timely, actionable leads from their Field Intelligence Groups.

In our field visits, ATF agents in Southwest border locations said that the investigative leads provided by ATF's Field Intelligence Groups are not timely, well developed, or actionable.[47] These complaints referred to leads developed by the Field Intelligence Group and to leads from developed by Industry Operations and forwarded by the Group. Field supervisors and agents told us they do not rely on their Group to generate investigative leads at all, opting instead to generate their own leads.

The most commonly stated criticism of the investigative leads from Field Intelligence Groups was that they were too old to be of value to agents conducting investigations. For example, field supervisors in one Southwest border field division told us the primary problem with the Field Intelligence Group leads is that the information is stale; one field supervisor said the Group forwards leads involving a time-to-crime of 1 to 3 years, but the

---

[46] In addition to visiting the Phoenix, Dallas, and Los Angeles Field Divisions during this review, we visited the Houston Field Division in June 2009 as part of our interim review of Project Gunrunner. During that visit, agents from the Houston Field Division also reported that investigative leads were not well-developed or actionable, although some of the complaints related specifically to investigative leads generated for the Gun Runner Impact Team initiative, which was under way at that time.

[47] Field Intelligence Groups support field agents in two ways: responding to direct requests for information from agents to support their cases, and proactive intelligence gathering to generate investigative leads to be referred to field agents. The criticisms expressed to the OIG concern these investigative leads. Agents we interviewed told us that when they requested information from their Field Intelligence Group to support a current case, they received a timely and useful response.

agents should be focusing on incidents with a time-to-crime of 3 to 6 months. Another field supervisor said the Field Intelligence Group will send him leads that can have a time-to-crime of up to 3 to 5 years. Although field personnel varied in what they considered a valuable time-to-crime, most cited a 1-year time-to-crime as the maximum threshold for a lead to be useful.

ATF field supervisors told us that the impact of receiving leads with an outdated time-to-crime is that agents waste time investigating the leads. For example, one field supervisor estimated that of about 25 investigative leads that the Field Intelligence Group sent to his enforcement group during 2009, only 1 or 2 warranted follow-up and neither of those leads resulted in any arrests or prosecutions. An agent in that enforcement group said that because the Field Intelligence Groups do not effectively screen leads, each lead that is assigned by a field supervisor requires an agent to spend time pursuing it and then to write a report in N-Force explaining that the lead did not pan out.

Field supervisors and agents said that they rely more on self-generated investigative leads and information from other sources to detect firearms trafficking activity. For example, some agents were using the weekly compilation of raw data on Mexican crime gun recovery and multiple sales data provided to the field directly from the National Tracing Center to conduct their own screening and analysis instead of using the Field Intelligence Groups.[48] ATF's National Firearms Trafficking Implementation Plan directs supervisors to review the multiple sales data to identify potential firearms traffickers "even though the [Field Intelligence Group] analyzes the data for trafficking leads against locally established criteria."[49] In September 2010, in response to a draft of this report, ATF told the OIG that field office personnel can quickly review the multiple sales data because they are more familiar with the local gun dealers, weapons of choice, and potential firearms trafficking suspects in their area, and they can request that Field Intelligence Group personnel conduct additional research. However, by generating their own investigative leads, agents may duplicate their Group's efforts. Agents also may use information that is less effective because they do not have access to the multiple sources used by Groups, and they do not have the time to conduct additional research that Group members should do before sending investigative leads to agents.

---

[48] Agents in the Dallas, Los Angeles, and Phoenix Field Divisions also reported that in addition to analyzing some of the same sources that the Field Intelligence Group uses, a primary source of their investigative leads was local gun dealers who call them to report suspicious activity and confidential informants, a type of source to which Field Intelligence Groups would not have access.

[49] ATF National Firearms Trafficking Enforcement Implementation Plan (June 25, 2009), 3.

ATF field agents also stated that some leads forwarded by a Field Intelligence Group as Project Gunrunner leads have no clear connection to firearms trafficking. A field supervisor provided the example of a Group-generated lead on a gang member in possession of one gun – which the supervisor does not consider to be a firearms trafficking offense – as a lead that was not useful. That supervisor said although there is no threshold for the number of guns associated with a purchaser, a useful investigative lead from the Group would involve a purchaser with at least two or three guns, or a suspect who illegally purchased guns with an out-of-state license. Another supervisor stated that the most useful intelligence for detecting firearms trafficking is information on the gun purchasers themselves – including the number and types of guns bought, the age and gender of the buyers, and background information indicating whether the buyers had the financial means to buy the guns.

Reporting multiple sales of handguns produces timely, actionable leads for detecting firearms trafficking.

The *Gun Control Act* requires that gun dealers report multiple sales of handguns (defined as two or more handguns sold at once or during any 5 consecutive business days) to ATF.[50] As discussed below, these multiple sales reports provide ATF with timely, actionable leads that can enable it to more quickly identify suspected firearms traffickers and disrupt their operations.[51] However, gun dealers are not required to report multiple sales of long guns to ATF.[52] Because long guns have become Mexican cartels' weapons of choice, multiple sales reporting has become less viable as a source of intelligence to disrupt the illegal flow of weapons to Mexico.

According to 18 U.S.C. § 923(g)(3), gun dealers must report multiple sales of handguns to their local ATF field office using a Report of Multiple Sales or Other Disposition of Pistols and Revolvers form (multiple sales report). Gun dealers must forward all multiple sales reports to the National Tracing Center by the close of business on the day that a reportable multiple sale occurs. The National Tracing Center enters the information on the multiple sales into ATF's tracing database (the Firearms Tracing System), which is subsequently made available to ATF field offices through

---

[50] 18 U.S.C. § 923(g)(3).

[51] For more information on potential indicators of trafficking by gun dealers, see Bruce Reinhart, "Implementing a Firearms Trafficking Strategy – Prosecuting Corrupt Federal Firearms Licensees," *United States Attorneys' Bulletin* (January 2002).

[52] Long guns include all variations of rifles and shotguns as defined in §§ 921(a)(5) to (8) of the *Gun Control Act*.

eTrace. If a trace request is matched to multiple sales report information, the trace can be completed in minutes rather than days or weeks.[53]

The purchase of multiple guns within a short period of time by an individual who is not a gun dealer may indicate that the individual is engaged in firearms trafficking. For example, firearms trafficking indicators include:

- multiple sales in which a purchaser also appears on one or more past gun traces;
- multiple sales in which the purchaser was born outside the United States;
- a multiple sale of five or more guns;
- more than one multiple sale at the same gun dealer on the same day;
- traces in which the recovered gun was purchased in a multiple sale; and
- crime guns traced back to a multiple sale in a state other than where a gun was recovered.

Additionally, ATF uses multiple sales reports to verify gun dealers' records, to detect suspicious activity, and to generate investigative leads. ATF personnel we interviewed in Southwest border offices cited multiple handgun sales data as a valuable source of timely and actionable investigative leads for detecting firearms trafficking and said such leads have led to the prosecution of traffickers.

Multiple sales reporting is a less viable source of intelligence on firearms traffickers because multiple sales of long guns are not reported.

Multiple sales of long guns are not subject to the same reporting requirements as handguns. Yet, long guns have become the Mexican cartels' weapons of choice. ATF reported in a statement to Congress last year:

> Until recently drug traffickers' "weapon of choice" had been .38 caliber handguns. However, they now have developed a preference for higher quality, more powerful weapons, such as

---

[53] If a gun is not a part of a multiple sales report, then the National Tracing Center uses the gun identifying information (such as the serial number and model) to determine the manufacturer or importer of the gun. The manufacturer or importer then can provide the name of the licensed gun dealer the first sold the gun. The National Tracing Center contacts that licensed gun dealer who checks their records to determine who the gun was first sold to. According to National Tracing Center staff, the length of time this process takes varies widely, but is usually about 7 to 10 days.

.223 and 7.62x39mm caliber rifles, 5.7x28 caliber rifles and pistols, and .50 caliber rifles; each of these types of weapons has been seized by ATF in route to Mexico.[54]

The OIG's analysis of National Tracing Center data of Mexican crime guns recovered from FY 2004 through FY 2009 confirmed the increase in the use of long guns by Mexican drug cartels. During this time, the percentage of crime guns recovered in Mexico that were long guns steadily increased each year from 20 percent in FY 2004 to 48 percent in FY 2009. By contrast, handguns represent a steadily decreasing portion of crime guns recovered in Mexico, dropping from 79 percent in FY 2004 to 50 percent in FY 2009. In FY 2009 long guns and handguns were recovered at almost the same rate.

Our analysis also found that long guns tend to have a shorter time-to-crime than handguns, and shorter time-to-crime intervals generate more valuable leads for ATF. According to Mexican crime gun data provided by ATF, of Mexican crime guns that were both sold for the first time and traced between December 1, 2006, and December 31, 2009, 973 were rifles (77 percent) and 279 were handguns (23 percent).

Evidence also indicates that Mexican cartels are obtaining long guns in multiple sales. The case study in the text box below demonstrates how high volumes of trafficked long guns can be obtained through multiple gun purchases. In that particular case, a trafficking ring purchased at least 336 weapons, of which the OIG determined through ATF data that 251 (75 percent) were long guns. Of the 251 long guns, all but 1 were purchased as a part of multiple sales, and these sales would have been reportable to ATF had they been handguns. According to ATF and other Department personnel, this case is one of many ATF cases involving multiple purchases of long guns.

While long guns are increasingly the Mexican cartels' preferred gun, there is no legal requirement in the United States to report multiple sales of these weapons. As a result, multiple sales reporting has become less viable to ATF as a source of intelligence to identify firearms trafficking organizations and disrupt the illegal flow of weapons to Mexico. For example, in the case described below, had there been a multiple sales reporting requirement on long guns, this case could have been initiated soon after March 13, 2006, when the first multiple purchase of a long gun took place (three AR-15 assault rifles along with two boxes of ammunition valued at $3,347). Instead, ATF did not initiate its investigation until mid-

---

[54] William Hoover, Assistant Director for Field Operations, ATF, before the Committee on the Judiciary Subcommittee on Crime and Drugs, U.S. Senate, concerning "Law Enforcement Responses to Mexican Drug Cartels" (March 17, 2009).

2007, over 1 year later, when ATF Industry Operations Investigators identified the trafficking ring through the inspection of a gun dealer.

A Case Study of a Firearms Trafficking Ring

In a statement to Congress on March 4, 2010, ATF's Deputy Director described a case in which straw purchasers bought and trafficked firearms for the Gulf Cartel in Mexico. The firearms trafficking ring consisted of 23 suspected traffickers who purchased guns and other gear out of Houston from March 13, 2006, to June 5, 2007. The ring purchased at least 336 firearms, of which 251 were long guns. These included .223, 7.62, and 5.7 caliber rifles. All but one of the long guns were purchased in multiple sales. For example, one of the suspects purchased 14 long guns, all weapons of choice, in 1 day from 1 firearms dealer. Of those 14 long guns, 2 were recovered in Mexico with a time-to-crime of under 2.5 years. Table 2 provides additional facts about this case.

Table 2: Impact of One Firearms Trafficking Ring

Suspects	23 suspects
Time frame	March 13, 2006, to June 5, 2007; 15 months
Purchases	96 purchases from 10 firearms dealers
Value	$367,419 total in merchandise, paid mostly in cash
Sales	Individual purchase totals ranged from $2,037 to $42,726
Firearms	336, plus ammunition, scopes, and other gear
Long guns	251 long guns purchased
Mexico recoveries	91 of the 336 total; 87 were long guns
Traces	21 of the 23 suspects have had traces linked to them
Time-to-crime	Median for the 87 long guns just under 1.5 years
Shortest	26 days
Longest	3 years 10 months
Deaths	57, including 18 law enforcement officers and civilians, plus 39 gunmen

Source: ATF Houston Field Division.

As of June 2010, ATF had shut down the firearms trafficking ring. Eleven of the traffickers had been convicted of various offenses, with sentences ranging from 3 months' to 8 years' imprisonment. The individual who was sentenced to 8 years had purchased firearms that were associated with eight murders in Mexico.

If multiple sales reporting of long guns was required, ATF would have had investigative leads to identify the trafficking ring earlier. Such reports also would have flagged the buyers' previous multiple purchases, and ATF could have sought cooperation from the straw purchasers to identify the Gulf Cartel members responsible.

Because reporting multiple sales of handguns generates timely, actionable investigative leads for Project Gunrunner, and because long guns have become Mexican cartels' weapons of choice, we believe that the reporting of multiple sales of long guns would assist ATF in identifying firearms trafficking suspects. Our analysis shows that many long guns seized in Mexico have a short time-to-crime and were often a part of a multiple purchase. We therefore believe that mandatory reporting of long gun multiple sales could help ATF identify, investigate, and refer for prosecution individuals who illegally traffic long guns into Mexico.

Recommendation

We recommend that ATF:

2. Work with the Department to explore options for seeking a requirement for reporting multiple sales of long guns.

Field Intelligence Groups lack consistent criteria for developing leads and have limited capability to monitor lead outcomes.

We examined how analysts in the Field Intelligence Groups process information to develop leads and how Group managers monitor the work of the analysts to assess the quality and usefulness of the leads they produce. As described in the following sections, there are no minimum national standards for Field Intelligence Groups to use in determining which leads to forward to agents, and the Groups in the four Southwest border field divisions vary in their development of localized standards for screening potential leads. Further, we found ATF's management information systems do not enable Field Intelligence Group managers to readily assess the outcomes of the leads sent to the criminal investigators for action.

ATF lacks clear criteria for Field Intelligence Groups to use in screening leads.

ATF has not established general guidelines or thresholds for Field Intelligence Groups to screen investigative leads to ensure that ATF agents receive only relevant leads that do not require agents to conduct further research. ATF Order 3700.2A, "Criminal Enforcement Intelligence Program Standard Operating Policies and Procedures" (October 2004), provides general guidance on reporting, collecting, maintaining, and disseminating criminal law enforcement and national security information, as well as intelligence staff responsibilities. However, the Order does not provide any guidelines for field intelligence personnel to follow in determining how to develop, screen, and analyze information to create actionable investigative leads for agents.

In February 2005 and again in February 2008, ATF issued criteria for referrals from Industry Operations and further required that management in each field division "meet and establish criteria for the type and scope of criminal information which is of interest to both ATF law enforcement and the [USAO]."[55] However, these criteria apply only to referrals generated by Industry Operations groups, not to referrals generated within the Field Intelligence Groups or by other entities. Similarly, ATF's National Firearms Trafficking Implementation Plan does not establish criteria for referrals generated within the Groups.

The most specific standards for investigative leads produced by Field Intelligence Groups are found in the *ATF Field Intelligence Group Supervisor's Guide Book*. The Guide Book states that Intelligence Research Specialists assigned to Groups are to collect, evaluate, and analyze intelligence to produce "finished tactical and operational analytical products."[56] These products are defined as an "analytical product resulting from cognitive effort wherein the intelligence research specialist explains findings, discloses links, recognizes patterns of activity, and makes predictions or recommendations." However, the Guide Book does not describe how field intelligence personnel are to do this.

We discussed with Southwest border Field Intelligence Group employees and supervisors how they determine what leads are of potential value to field agents in the absence of agency criteria for them to use in determining how to handle leads. They use some type of threshold to determine whether a lead should be forwarded to field agents, or not forwarded, but the thresholds were primarily focused on Industry Operations referrals and were not tailored to the needs of the enforcement groups served by Field Intelligence Groups. Specifically:

1. The Dallas Field Division established written criteria for screening referrals of information from Industry Operations in January 2006 in response to ATF instruction to do so.
2. The Phoenix Field Division established a written plan and criteria to screen referrals of information from Industry Operations In February 2009.
3. The Houston Field Intelligence Group did not have written criteria for screening referrals of information from Industry Operations but reported using a list of six factors to determine which to refer to agents.
4. The Los Angeles Field Division reported that it did not have criteria at the time of our site visit in January 2010, but subsequently developed "referral criteria" on the types of violations and

---

[55] Assistant Director, Enforcement Programs and Services, ATF memorandum to all Special Agents in Charge and all Directors, Industry Operations, Referrals of Information, February 22, 2005, and *ATF Industry Operations Handbook,* Handbook 5030.2C (February 2008), 117.

[56] ATF, *Field Intelligence Group Supervisor's Guide Book* (September 2009), Appendix.

information that must be referred to agents through the Field Intelligence Group.

Only one Group (the Dallas Field Division) included criteria designed to screen out leads that did not meet the prosecutorial guidelines of the division's USAOs.

We concluded that the field divisions did not provide sufficient guidance to intelligence personnel about how to develop and screen intelligence to meet the requirements of the enforcement groups. Two field supervisors and Field Intelligence Group members we interviewed cited a variety of standards for determining whether particular pieces of information should be forwarded to enforcement groups as leads. For example, one Intelligence Research Specialist cited three criteria used by her Group to ensure that investigative leads sent to field offices are valuable, emphasizing that the goal is to forward only "actionable" intelligence, which she defined as "information that could help an agent in some way." The criteria cited by that Intelligence Research Specialist were that leads be: (1) original, meaning not already under investigation by another office; (2) timely – so that the agent can be relatively assured that the suspect is still retrievable; and (3) of federal interest, with leads that are better suited for state and local law enforcement referred there rather than to ATF field offices.

A member of a different Field Intelligence Group stated that the goal is to give agents as much information as possible about a suspect. That Group member said that he relies on his instincts and considers factors such as the time-to-crime of a gun trace. He also stated that if the time-to-crime is within 2 years he automatically sends the lead, but if it is older than 2 years, he may not. We noted that this is not consistent with the need for more recent time-to-crime leads generally described to us by agents. A Group supervisor in another division stated that the analysts are expected to use discretion when screening information to eliminate the "white noise" and provide the most relevant information to the field.

Some Field Intelligence Group supervisors and members told us that they knew some leads they provided had no likely investigative value to agents. One supervisor commented, "A lot of times, the agents in the field can't work that referral . . . most likely it won't lead to a prosecution . . . ." That supervisor believed the information to be valuable nonetheless because it added to other information that the agents are receiving. Regarding the time-to-crime of a gun trace, the supervisor said the Group forwards investigative leads to the field on any gun recovered in Mexico with a time-to-crime of 1 year or less. An Intelligence Research Specialist assigned to that Group told us that referrals sent to field agents are often not adequate and have little investigative potential when the time-to-crime is longer than

1 year. Other Group members who said that some leads on Mexican crime guns had no investigative value stated that many of those leads were based on information that was outdated when the Group received it.

Field Intelligence Group managers cannot effectively monitor the quality or status of Industry Operations leads referred to enforcement groups.

In discussing the quality of leads with Field Intelligence Group supervisors, we found that they have limited capability to monitor the referrals they receive from Industry Operations and to obtain feedback on the results of leads their Groups provide to agents.[57] ATF requires Field Intelligence Groups to monitor the timeliness of their processing of referrals they receive from Industry Operations, including whether they accept or reject each referral, and to provide quarterly reports on the status of referrals. The Groups are also required to monitor the status of referrals that are accepted and forwarded to enforcement groups. Enforcement groups receiving referrals from Field Intelligence Groups are required to annotate in N-Force, within 30 days, if no investigative activity has occurred. This is so that field offices, which have access to N-Force, can assess their effectiveness through performance measures such as how many referrals were made under which statute, the number of criminal cases initiated because of referrals, and case outcomes. ATF further emphasized the importance of referrals in the 2009 National Firearms Trafficking Implementation Plan by adding a performance measure to evaluate the quality of referrals sent to Criminal Enforcement.

However, both Field Intelligence Group supervisors and Industry Operations Area Supervisors told us that tracking the disposition of referrals and providing feedback is cumbersome because ATF's enforcement and industry operations databases (N-Force and N-Spect) are not integrated and because agents can access only N-Force and Industry Operations Investigators can access only N-Spect. The Chief of ATF's Office of Strategic Management, which is responsible for ATF data management, stated that because the N-Spect and N-Force systems are not linked electronically, when Industry Operations makes a referral to Criminal Enforcement, the referral is made "off line" – by e-mail, hand delivery, or regular mail. After the referral is made, the N-Spect file is closed, and there is generally no reporting on the progress of the referral.

Because the referral process is not automated, each referral is forwarded on a printed form, and Field Intelligence Group supervisors track

---

[57] ATF Order 3700.2A defines intelligence feedback as "interaction between consumers of finished intelligence and the producers to help intelligence managers evaluate the effectiveness of intelligence support, identify intelligence gaps, and focus more precisely on consumer needs."

referrals using individually developed spreadsheets into which they enter information. This information includes the date of the lead, its source (Industry Operations or other), the enforcement group to which it was sent, and the status of the lead – that is, whether it was closed or an agent was assigned to it and pursued the lead. To obtain outcome data for the spreadsheets, the supervisors search N-Force and manually retrieve the data, which some said was time-consuming. For example, one Group supervisor told us that to produce the required quarterly status reports, he must search all "open" referrals in N-Force, update the disposition field for every active referral on his spreadsheet, and forward the updated spreadsheet to the Industry Operations Area Supervisor. That supervisor in turn must access N-Spect and update the disposition of each open referral in that system.

In addition, we observed that the information in Field Intelligence Group supervisors' spreadsheets did not contain feedback from enforcement groups about the *utility* of the investigative leads the Group provided, whether from Industry Operations or leads developed by the Field Intelligence Group itself. Agents enter information into N-Force using drop-down menus that contain generic reasons for closure of a lead. The agents can also provide specific feedback on the lead in an open comment field. However, we were told that agents did not often enter into N-Force the specific reasons that a lead was not useful, such as why it did not meet prosecutorial guidelines or how it could have been improved. Some field personnel told us that they may request specific feedback on their leads directly from agents and field supervisors, particularly in offices where the agents and Groups are co-located. Nonetheless, we concluded that tracked information was not effective in allowing the Group supervisors or members to assess the utility of the leads they provided to agents or to provide Industry Operations with specific feedback on their referrals.

The difficulty of determining referral outcomes was demonstrated by the efforts ATF undertook to provide the OIG with a limited sample of the outcome of Industry Operations referrals to Criminal Enforcement through Field Intelligence Groups. In December 2009, we requested the number of Industry Operations referrals to Criminal Enforcement through Field Intelligence Groups from FY 2004 through FY 2009, and their outcomes (whether the referrals were accepted and how many resulted in a criminal investigation). In April 2010, ATF headquarters provided data that indicated 5,106 referrals were made by the four field division Field Intelligence Groups in the stated period. We determined that 476 of those referrals were (1) firearms-related, (2) referred within ATF, and (3) shown as "accepted" in

N-Force.[58] In May 2010, we asked the Office of Strategic Management to provide us the N-Force case management log entries for a random sample of 213 cases. That data was finally provided on August 4, 2010.

When asked why the process had taken so long, the Chief of ATF's Office of Strategic Management, which is responsible for ATF data management, stated it took months to research and to document the specific referral outcomes because of limits in ATF's case management system. Staff in ATF's Field Operations Office had to research each individual referral to locate and document the outcome information. The Chief stated that ATF has annually sought funding needed to modernize its case management system, but that the requests have been disapproved.[59]

Recommendations

We recommend that ATF:

3. Ensure that each Southwest border firearms trafficking enforcement group develops and regularly updates guidelines for their Field Intelligence Group that specify the most useful types of investigative leads.

4. Develop an automated process that enables ATF managers to track and evaluate the usefulness of investigative leads provided to firearms trafficking enforcement groups.

ATF intelligence personnel are not adequately sharing firearms trafficking information with each other to develop or enhance intelligence to further investigations.

Despite the importance of intelligence to Project Gunrunner's mission, we found that sharing of firearms trafficking-related information and techniques among intelligence personnel in Southwest border locations and in the Mexico Country Office is limited.

---

[58] We excluded referrals sent to other federal, state, and local law enforcement agencies as these entities are not required to provide ATF with status reports on the outcomes of the referrals.

[59] Budget documents show that ATF has requested funds to improve various N-Force and N-Spect capabilities since at least FY 2004. In its FY 2012 budget request, ATF requested $3.3 million for this purpose. Proposed improvements include providing a single entry point for all investigative and inspection information and reducing data redundancy. As of August 2010, ATF had not received funds to upgrade N-Force and N-Spect for this purpose.

<u>Routine sharing of information among intelligence personnel is limited</u>.

ATF Order 3700.2A directs Intelligence Research Specialists to "routinely interact with their counterparts in other field divisions, and conduct liaison with analysts from other law enforcement agencies and the Office of Strategic Intelligence and Information."[60] The ATF Office of Strategic Intelligence and Information subsequently created an Intelligence Collection Plan to establish information collection and exchange procedures for Project Gunrunner, including intelligence that may be shared with Mexican officials. The Plan states that to develop "real-time, actionable intelligence relating to firearms trafficking networks operating in both the United States and Mexico," ATF field offices will establish procedures to collect information from a variety of sources, including "exchanging information with other ATF field offices . . . ." ATF's National Firearms Trafficking Enforcement Implementation Plan, sent from the Acting Assistant Director (Field Operations) to all Special Agents in Charge on June 25, 2009, mandated that the Intelligence Collection Plan be provided to, and "thoroughly reviewed by," all Field Intelligence Group personnel by July 31, 2009. ATF also established the requirement for Field Intelligence Group communications in its June 2007 Gunrunner strategy, which stated, "ATF [Field Intelligence Groups] need to coordinate inter- and intra-division intelligence activities much like operational activities."[61]

During our fieldwork, we interviewed 11 intelligence personnel in Southwest border field divisions and Mexico City, as well as 4 of their supervisors. We determined through those interviews that routine communication between Field Intelligence Groups primarily occurs at the supervisory level. Southwest border Field Intelligence Group supervisors participate in quarterly teleconferences with their counterparts in the Western region and ATF headquarters intelligence personnel from the Office of Strategic Intelligence and Information to share information on investigations and trends related to firearms trafficking. The supervisors also told us that, although each Group pursues cases separately, the supervisors contact each other when they need to and share information pertaining to cases or investigative referrals with other Field Intelligence Groups. However, we determined that non-supervisory Group members do not participate in these exchanges.

Non-supervisory intelligence personnel in these offices told us that they rarely receive information from their counterparts in other Southwest border field divisions and that they communicate with these counterparts

---

[60] ATF Order 3700.2A, "Criminal Enforcement Intelligence Program Standard Operating Policies and Procedures" (October 2004), 12.

[61] ATF, *Southwest Border Initiative: Project Gunrunner* (June 2007), I-13.

infrequently. In addition to the lack of communication across Field Intelligence Groups, non-supervisory staff members told us there is limited interaction and poor communication internal to the field division – both among Field Intelligence Group members and with non-Group members working on Project Gunrunner, such as agents and Industry Operations Investigators. In our interviews, we were told that intelligence personnel are typically excluded from meetings with agents. An Intelligence Research Specialist in one Field Intelligence Group said the Specialists are not included in meetings with agents and do not receive the information they need to effectively support the cases the agents are working on. This Specialist stated that the Intelligence Research Specialists should not be overlooked by agents as they perform additional research to supplement the information provided to agents to support their cases.

An Intelligence Research Specialist in another Field Intelligence Group said that because personnel working on Project Gunrunner – including agents, Intelligence Research Specialists, and Industry Operations Investigators – do not all communicate, they do not understand each other's responsibilities. Further, she said intelligence personnel were missing opportunities to regularly share firearms trafficking-related information and analytical techniques with their intelligence peers that they told us would be useful to them.

Field Intelligence Group supervisors, Office of Strategic Intelligence and Information staff, and Mexico Country Office personnel also told us that they believed there is a need for more communication between Field Intelligence Groups. For example, a Southwest border Group supervisor stated that it would be beneficial to have one-on-one meetings between Field Intelligence Group supervisors and the Intelligence Research Specialists working on Project Gunrunner cases to discuss the available information and to coordinate with each other. Similarly, Office of Strategic Intelligence and Information officials told us that Field Intelligence Groups are responsible for communication and deconfliction across divisions and therefore the Groups need to increase the information flow between them. An Assistant Attaché in ATF's Mexico Country Office also stated that communication between Southwest border Field Intelligence Group personnel needed to be improved to increase the flow of information to Mexico.

We were told by Southwest border intelligence personnel that non-supervisory intelligence personnel have not been included in cross-division Field Intelligence Group conferences. Intelligence Research Specialists we interviewed stated that attending such conferences would enable them to, for example, identify regional and national needs, inform ATF managers what resources the intelligence personnel need to accomplish their job, and allow the personnel to share best practices. Several Group members stated that this type of collaboration with each other would help the Groups to operate more efficiently and to better support agents' needs.

ATF officials told us of two recent conferences held by the Office of Strategic Intelligence and Information. The first was a national Field Intelligence Group conference in August 2009 with an agenda that included intelligence requirements and analysis of firearms trafficking. However, that conference was limited to Group supervisors, Assistant Special Agents in Charge, and Special Agents in Charge. Non-supervisory intelligence personnel were excluded. The second national Field Intelligence Group conference, held in August 2010, included non-supervisory intelligence personnel, but ATF officials told us the conference was not focused on Project Gunrunner or Southwest border issues.

ATF border liaisons are not effectively coordinating with ATF's Mexico Country Office.

The Border Liaison Program is a key element of Project Gunrunner's information sharing strategy. ATF's June 2007 Project Gunrunner strategy states that each Southwest border field division will assign a special agent to act as border liaison in the respective division area of operation. The strategy states that border liaisons "will be the front line of [the Project Gunrunner] initiative, attacking the issues on the ground level. In their areas of operation, they will be responsible for driving the collection and subsequent dissemination of actionable investigative intelligence through the Project Gunrunner structure."[62]

Designated border liaisons in each Southwest border field division are required by ATF's Intelligence Collection Plan to share firearms trafficking intelligence with both EPIC and the Mexico Country Office. Further, ATF's Gunrunner strategy states that all ATF activities in Mexico should be coordinated through the Mexico Country Office at the U.S. Embassy in Mexico City. The Gunrunner strategy states that "failure to coordinate all ATF official activities can cause serious problems for all personnel in country and for TDY personnel requiring country clearance or other diplomatic assistance."[63] Mexico Country Office staff also stated that it is vital for them to be aware of all discussions and agreements between border liaisons and Mexican officials so that ATF's position and response are uniform.

However, we found the border liaisons were not effectively coordinating with the ATF Mexico Country Office. Staff in the Mexico

---

[62] ATF, *Southwest Border Initiative: Project Gunrunner* (June 2007), 12.

[63] ATF, *Southwest Border Initiative: Project Gunrunner* (June 2007), 5.

Country Office told us that border liaisons had frequently been traveling back and forth to Mexico and holding discussions with Mexican officials without the required coordination.[64] We were told that key firearms trafficking intelligence collected by border liaisons and outcomes of meetings between border liaisons and Mexican officials were not consistently shared with the ATF Mexico Country Office, which created problems. For example, border liaisons told Mexican officials that ATF would be able to provide them with requested training, but the Office was unaware of the obligation and unable to provide the training. Mexico Country Office staff told us, "We want to make sure we can deliver what's promised to the Mexicans. It's a coordination issue."[65]

Another ATF Assistant Attaché described the border liaison process as "disjointed" and informal. He noted that the Border Liaison Program is new for ATF and that ATF officials "need to work the kinks out." Although he explained that the border liaisons contact him when they need something, he told us that some field divisions' liaisons are more proactive than others. Yet another Assistant Attaché told us he does not even know who the border liaisons are in ATF or what they are doing and he "never hears from them."

ATF Mexico Country Office officials told us that they believe the problems stemmed from a lack of direction governing the information exchange and communication protocols for border liaisons. One Assistant Attaché said he has tried on multiple occasions to convene a meeting with all border liaisons to devise a strategy for intelligence exchange between the border liaisons and the Mexico Country Office, but has not been successful. That Assistant Attaché said, "[Mexico Country Office] has an overall strategy in Mexico and would like to have an overall strategy ATF-wide . . . then [border liaisons] would fit within that strategy." According to the Mexico Country Office, a coordinated approach has been difficult to develop because the liaisons report to their respective field divisions, while the Mexico Country Office is organizationally aligned under the International Affairs Office at ATF headquarters.

---

[64] Border liaisons told us they often coordinate with the Mexico Country Office representative at the location closest to them. For example, the border liaison in the San Diego Field Office might contact the Assistant Attaché assigned to the consulate in Tijuana, Mexico.

[65] During our site visit in March 2010, Mexico Country Office staff indicated that ATF created rules requiring border liaisons to contact Mexico City in advance of any travel to Mexico and that since the rules were established, communications have improved. However, when we inquired about those rules, the Chief of ATF's International Affairs Office reported that ATF does not currently have a directive addressing border liaisons but that border liaisons will be addressed in a Foreign Operations Order, which was still being drafted as of July 2010.

We examined the direction given to the border liaisons and found that one reason for the lack of coordination may be that the duties of the border liaison position have not been well defined. Only the Phoenix Field Division has established a written description of qualifications and responsibilities for its border liaisons. According to that description, prior to any meetings in Mexico the border liaisons were to advise their supervisors of the intended travel and receive prior approval from their Assistant Special Agent in Charge or Special Agent in Charge. The description states that it is the Phoenix Field Division's responsibility to ensure that the Mexico Country Office is made aware of any significant liaison activities in Mexico prior to assistance being rendered. The description also requires liaisons to document their activities in N-Force at the end of each month for review and to forward the information to the Mexico Country Office and International Affairs Office (at ATF headquarters). ATF provided us no additional information on the roles or responsibilities of its border liaison personnel at other Southwest border field divisions.

In sum, we found that ATF has not established minimum expectations for border liaisons' information sharing role with the government of Mexico, the ATF Mexico Country Office, or within their own field divisions. While variation in the role of liaisons in different field divisions is to be expected, we believe that ATF should establish minimum expectations for the border liaisons to ensure that they effectively coordinate their actions in Mexico with ATF's Mexico Country Office.

Recommendations

We recommend that ATF:

5. Develop and implement procedures for Southwest border intelligence personnel to routinely exchange intelligence-related information in accordance with ATF Order 3700.2A and the Intelligence Collection Plan.

6. Develop a method for Southwest border intelligence personnel to regularly share analytical techniques and best practices pertaining to Project Gunrunner.

7. Formalize a position description that establishes minimum expectations regarding the roles and responsibilities of border liaisons.

ATF has not focused its enforcement efforts on complex conspiracy investigations with multiple defendants, which are the type of cases that can best disrupt firearms trafficking rings. Further, ATF is not fully utilizing the OCDETF Program to investigate complex conspiracy firearms trafficking-related Project Gunrunner cases. Because firearms trafficking is not specifically prohibited by any federal statute, when ATF does identify trafficking operations, it must use other charges – such as providing false information on a federal form – that may be difficult to prove, result in fewer prosecutions by USAOs, or carry low penalties. As a result, USAOs often decline ATF's cases that are based on the most commonly used statutes at a higher rate than other Project Gunrunner cases.

Project Gunrunner's focus has remained on gun dealer inspections and straw purchaser investigations rather than targeting higher-level traffickers, smugglers, and recipients of firearms.

As in other types of organized crime, leaders of firearms trafficking rings typically conspire to commit a series of crimes and deploy lower-level members to carry out those crimes. Although Project Gunrunner has initiated and referred more individual cases for prosecution, as discussed in Part I of this report, those cases mostly involve straw purchasers and corrupt gun dealers, not those who organize and command the trafficking operations. ATF does not measure the number of complex conspiracy cases it initiates or refers for prosecution, but our analysis found that 68 percent of Project Gunrunner cases referred to USAOs for prosecution through the end of FY 2009 were single defendant cases. ATF personnel in one field division told us that they felt that their management discouraged them from conducting the kinds of complex conspiracy cases that can target higher-level members of trafficking rings.

Firearms trafficking conspiracies can involve multiple violations of U.S. law.

Although no federal law specifically prohibits firearms trafficking, the members of trafficking rings typically violate federal firearms and export laws when obtaining and smuggling guns to Mexico. Straw purchasers commit a criminal act by lying on the federal Firearms Transaction Record (Form 4473), which requires purchasers to certify that they are not buying the guns on behalf of others before a gun dealer can sell them the guns. "Prohibited persons" commit criminal acts by obtaining weapons at gun shows that they are not allowed to possess because, for example, they have criminal convictions or are illegal or nonimmigrant aliens.[66] The act of paying others to illegally purchase and supply guns also is a violation of 18 U.S.C. § 922(a)(1)(A), which is one of the most common statutes under which ATF's Project Gunrunner cases are prosecuted, as discussed later in this Part of the report. Smuggling illegally obtained guns across the border into Mexico is a violation of 18 U.S.C. § 554, a statute under which ICE cases are typically prosecuted.[67] And while the violent criminal activities of the cartels in Mexico do not fall under U.S. law, the United States can extradite traffickers from Mexico and prosecute them for any crimes they have committed in the United States.

Although the members of firearms trafficking rings typically conspire to commit crimes in the United States when obtaining and smuggling guns to Mexico, we found that Project Gunrunner is aimed primarily at the initial sellers and purchasers of guns, not at those who direct and most profit from the trafficking. USAO and ATF personnel we interviewed stated that Project Gunrunner cases rarely pursue those who request and pay for the guns. Although typically these cases pursue one or two suspects, others – including those orchestrating the conspiracy – usually escape prosecution. This low-level investigative focus is discussed in ATF's 2009 National Firearms Trafficking Enforcement Strategy and the accompanying Implementation Plan, which emphasize investigations of gun dealers with firearms trafficking indicators, gun shows, flea markets, unlicensed dealers, and straw purchasers.

ATF has not focused enforcement efforts on complex conspiracy cases involving multiple defendants.

The OIG's analysis of all Project Gunrunner cases that ATF referred to USAOs for prosecution from FY 2004 through FY 2009 found that the majority (68 percent) involved only 1 defendant (see Table 3). Only 5 percent of the cases had more than 6 defendants, and 2 percent had more than 10 defendants. Overall, the average number of defendants per case was 2.03.

---

[66] 18 U.S.C. § 922(g) lists nine categories of prohibited persons.

[67] 18 U.S.C. § 554 states that whoever fraudulently or knowingly exports or sends from the United States, or attempts to export or send from the United States, any merchandise, article, or object contrary to any law or regulation of the United States, or receives, conceals, buys, sells, or in any manner facilitates the transportation, concealment, or sale of such merchandise, article or object, prior to exportation, knowing the same to be intended for exportation contrary to any law or regulation of the United States, shall be fined under this title, imprisoned not more than 10 years, or both.

Table 3: ATF Project Gunrunner Cases and Defendants

	Number of Cases	Percentage of Cases
Cases with 1 defendant	693	68%
Cases with 2 defendants	150	15%
Cases with 3-5 defendants	118	12%
Cases with 6-10 defendants	35	3%
Cases with more than 10 defendants	19	2%
Totals	**1,015**	**100%**

Source: ATF N-Force data.

AUSAs in Southwest border locations told us that directing the efforts of Project Gunrunner toward building larger, multi-defendant conspiracy cases would better disrupt the trafficking organizations. For example, one AUSA discussed the benefit of pursuing the top of the trafficking organizations, although he said he did not receive many of those cases from ATF. He stated:

> Are there 15 or 20 guys told to go out and buy 1 gun [each] which are [then] collected at one point? Can we find that collector, the one who is actually gathering up the stuff? Where is the money coming from? . . . If you answer those questions, then you can start making some progress in terms of fighting guns going south.

Other AUSAs told the OIG that they also had a strong preference for larger, complex conspiracy cases.

In our interviews with agents in one Southwest border field division, we found that a contributing factor to ATF's lack of multi-defendant cases was the approach of field supervisors. ATF staff in this field division told us they felt discouraged from conducting complex conspiracy cases. Agents we interviewed told us that after investigating the lower ranking members of a firearms trafficking ring, cases are often closed and referred for prosecution. These agents stated that they believe this practice limited their ability to pursue higher level cases and resulted in cases being opened and closed quickly, with less regard to the significance or outcome of the cases.

We asked the ATF Special Agent in Charge of that field division about pursuing these higher level cases. He acknowledged that he preferred his agents to initiate cases that could be completed within 1 month rather than cases that involve surveillance, wiretaps, and other investigative methods typical of complex conspiracy cases.

One Field Intelligence Group supervisor told us that Project Gunrunner is not seeking information to conduct proactive investigations and producing complex conspiracy cases for prosecution. According to this supervisor, ATF should conduct its investigations "with the mindset of not only 'you [the suspects] are guilty of this,' but 'Where did you get that gun?'" He went on to say, "If we know that specific individuals . . . are hiring straw purchasers . . . we can target them, do surveillance on them, build a conspiracy case, and go after them."

After we provided a draft of this report to ATF, ATF issued a strategy document, entitled "Project Gunrunner – A Cartel Focused Strategy" (September 2010 cartel strategy), to revise its approach to combating firearms trafficking to Mexico and related violence. ATF distributed the strategy document to ATF field personnel and International Affairs Office staff on September 16, 2010. In this document ATF acknowledged the limitations of ATF's historical investigative focus on straw purchasers and corrupt gun dealers and stated that ATF would "place greater emphasis on multi-defendant conspiracy cases that focus on persons who organize, direct, and finance cartel-related firearms and explosives trafficking operations."[68]

Recommendation

We recommend that ATF:

8. Focus on developing more complex conspiracy cases against higher level gun traffickers and gun trafficking conspirators.

Project Gunrunner has not made full use of the OCDETF Program's resources to conduct more complex conspiracy investigations.

ATF's Project Gunrunner investigations generally have not been conducted in coordination with the Department's multi-agency Organized Crime Drug Enforcement Task Force (OCDETF) Program, which often targets drug organizations. Although ATF has achieved some good results when coordinating with OCDETF, we found that ATF's focus on fast investigations as well as management and staff misunderstandings about how the OCDETF Program works have created barriers to greater coordination.

The OIG's analysis of ATF case data illustrated ATF's underutilization of the OCDETF Program. Of the 374 Project Gunrunner cases that ATF

---

[68] ATF, "Project Gunrunner – A Cartel Focused Strategy" (September 2010), 4.

closed in FY 2009, only 8 percent (30 cases) were designated as OCDETF.[69] We also found that when ATF referred OCDETF cases to USAOs for prosecution, the cases resulted in much longer sentences than non-OCDETF cases. The 30 Project Gunrunner cases designated as OCDETF resulted in an average sentence of 80 months. In comparison, the average sentence for all Project Gunrunner cases from FY 2004 through FY 2009 was 33 months. Similarly, the average number of defendants differed sharply. While the average number of defendants for the 30 OCDETF cases was 6, the average number of defendants for all Project Gunrunner cases was just 2.

ATF previously has directed staff to use the OCDETF Program, and the Department now requires that the OCEDETF Program be used for cases involving Mexican drug cartels.

ATF policy has directed field staff to use the OCDETF Program since at least July 2005, and in ATF's June 2007 Gunrunner strategy, ATF emphasized using OCDETF for appropriate firearms trafficking cases.[70] According to the Gunrunner strategy, "OCDETF assets will be sought at the earliest possible time once a qualifying nexus to a known [drug trafficking organization] is documented."[71] Further, in April 2009, the Associate Deputy Attorney General serving as the Director of the OCDETF Program issued a memorandum stating that firearms trafficking cases are eligible for the OCDETF Program. He stated:

> Investigations principally targeting firearms trafficking, rather than the underlying drug trafficking, are eligible for OCDETF designation if there is a sufficient nexus between the firearms and a major Mexican drug trafficking organization, provided the investigation otherwise meets OCDETF case standards.[72]

Despite this emphasis, in the 15-month period following the memorandum, ATF reported that it has opened only 11 OCDETF cases related to the firearms trafficking activities of Mexican drug cartels.

---

[69] ATF was the lead agency in 21 percent (768 of 3,671) of all OCDETF cases in which ATF participated from FY 2004 through FY 2009.

[70] ATF Order 3530.3, Organized Crime Drug Enforcement Task Force Program (July 2005), and ATF Southwest Border Initiative Project Gunrunner (June 2007).

[71] ATF, *Southwest Border Initiative: Project Gunrunner* (June 2007), 12.

[72] Stuart G. Nash, Associate Deputy Attorney General and Director of OCDETF, memorandum to OCDETF Regional Agency and AUSA Coordinators, Lead Task Force Attorneys, Executive Assistants, and Washington Agency Representatives Group, Guidelines for Consideration of OCDETF Designation for Firearms Trafficking Cases Related to Mexican Drug Cartels, April 27, 2009.

In January 2010, the Deputy Attorney General required ATF and other Department components to use the OCDETF Program for all activities targeting the Mexican cartels as part of the Department's strategy for combating the cartels (cartel strategy). The cartel strategy specifically identified combating firearms trafficking as a key objective, named Project Gunrunner as the primary ATF initiative in achieving that objective, and stated that "increasingly close collaboration between ATF and the efforts of the multi-agency drug task forces along the border, including, most particularly, the OCDETF co-located Strike Forces, ensures that scarce ATF resources are directed at the most important targets."[73]

ATF's use of the OCDETF Program is limited by ATF's focus on fast investigations, misunderstandings about the program, and low numbers of ATF staff assigned to OCDETF task forces.

We found that three factors have limited ATF's use of the OCDETF Program in the past – ATF's focus on fast investigations, misunderstandings about how the OCDETF Program operates, and ATF supervisors assigning few or no staff to OCDETF task forces.

The same ATF agents in the Southwest border field division who reported that they felt discouraged from pursuing complex conspiracy cases told us that field supervisors generally discouraged OCDETF cases because the supervisors favored faster investigations. For example, an agent we interviewed from a firearms trafficking enforcement group described "taking a lot of heat" for having taken a case to the OCDETF Program. The agent said that ATF field management had previously turned down a number of cases that might have been proposed for OCDETF consideration. The agent said that not using the OCDETF Program has resulted in agents not pursuing the "higher people in the food chain" of the trafficking rings.

The OIG asked an ATF official responsible for coordinating ATF's participation in the OCDETF Program why ATF field staff were reluctant to use the program. The official expressed concern that staff across the Southwest border, especially managers, incorrectly believed that a case could be counted as a Project Gunrunner or an OCDETF case for the purposes of ATF's performance measures, but not both. As a result, managers were reluctant to take cases to OCDETF. The official said the reluctance was continuing despite the Deputy Attorney General's 2010 cartel strategy and 2009 direction from the OCDETF Executive Council to use OCDETF against drug cartels' firearms trafficking.

---

[73] David W. Ogden, Deputy Attorney General, memorandum to heads of Department components and all United States Attorneys, Strategy for Combating the Mexican Cartels, January 7, 2010.

We also found that some ATF agents misunderstood the requirements of the OCDETF Program in ways that may have contributed to the low number of OCDETF-Gunrunner cases. In September 2010, ATF told the OIG that, prior to the April 2009 OCDETF Director's memorandum, ATF firearms trafficking investigations with no significant drug trafficking nexus were frequently refused by the OCDETF Program. However, our review found that even after the April 2009 memorandum, some agents still believed that OCDETF cases must be brought mainly against persons and organizations on the Department's priority drug target list.[74] Other ATF agents indicated that they did not believe that AUSAs would be interested in OCDETF cases involving firearms trafficking, rather than drug trafficking. For example, one field supervisor said he believed that to present an OCDETF case, ATF agents "better have a DEA guy or an ICE guy sitting next to them." ATF agents said that ATF senior management needed to send a clarification to all field staff instructing them to fully implement the Deputy Attorney General's cartel strategy.

We also noted that in some locations, ATF supervisors have assigned few or no staff to OCDETF task forces operating in their areas. For example, in McAllen, Texas – a center of firearms trafficking activity where ATF has two enforcement groups, including one dedicated to Project Gunrunner – ATF has only two agents in the OCDETF satellite office. In San Diego, where ATF has three enforcement teams, one of which is dedicated to Project Gunrunner, only one agent is assigned to the OCDETF task force. In Laredo, Texas, ATF has no agents assigned to the OCDETF task force.

In contrast, ATF's Phoenix Field Division has an enforcement group (up to 10 agents) assigned to and co-located with the Phoenix OCDETF task force. Through one ongoing case from that task force, the ATF agents indicted four people and identified a suspect in Mexico as the head of the trafficking ring. The supervisor of that enforcement group said, "If it is a bigger case that's going to [succeed] on the border, there is a good chance you are going to spend some money," and that OCDETF was an important way to obtain the resources needed for complex conspiracy investigations. Other ATF staff we interviewed told us that through OCDETF task forces they can obtain intelligence from other agencies, particularly the DEA, on drug cartels' firearms trafficking activity, helping ATF to investigate firearms trafficking rings, not just straw purchasers.

We asked ATF officials why they had not assigned more staff to OCDETF task forces. ATF responded that it makes decisions based on

---

[74] The Department maintains a unified list of international "command and control" drug traffickers and money launderers called the Consolidated Priority Organization Target list.

where it sees "cases of firearms trafficking or violations of other federal firearm laws more pronounced and where they can maximize results of affecting violent crime. [75]"

According to an ATF official responsible for ATF's participation in the OCDETF Program, in the past, ATF has consistently requested more funding from the OCDETF Program to cover additional agents that ATF assigns to OCDETF cases. However, the official said that the requests have been rejected by the Department's Justice Management Division or the White House Office of Management and Budget.

In its September 2010 cartel strategy document, ATF emphasized the advantages of using OCDETF as a part of its efforts to impede firearms trafficking to Mexico. The memorandum that accompanied the strategy document stated, "At the heart of our increased emphasis on cartel focused investigations is greater use of the [OCDETF] program" and the strategy itself directed all field offices to "consider assigning a complement of special agents" to the OCDETF task forces.[76]

Recommendation

We recommend that ATF:

9. Send guidance to field management, agents, and intelligence staff encouraging them to participate in and exploit the resources and tools of the OCDETF Program, as directed in the Deputy Attorney General's Cartel Strategy.

Statutes used to combat firearms trafficking do not have strong penalties.

There is no federal statute specifically prohibiting firearms trafficking or straw purchases. Consequently, ATF agents and federal prosecutors use other criminal statutes to charge individuals involved in firearms trafficking crimes. These statutes carry relatively low sentences, particularly for straw purchasers of guns. The Sentencing Guidelines also provide short sentences for firearms trafficking-related crimes. As a result, individuals

---

[75] As of September 2010, ATF reported that, in addition to the task force in Phoenix, it had an enforcement group (12 personnel) assigned to the Houston OCDETF task force and 1 agent each assigned to OCDETF task forces in El Paso, Texas, and Tucson, Arizona.

[76] Mark R. Chait, Assistant Director for Field Operations, memorandum to all Assistant Directors and Field Operations Personnel, Project Gunrunner – A Cartel Focused Strategy, September 8, 2010, and ATF, "Project Gunrunner – A Cartel Focused Strategy" (September 2010), 10.

convicted under these statutes generally receive lower penalties than persons convicted of other types of trafficking.

__In the absence of a specific federal statute, ATF uses a wide variety of statutes to address criminal firearms trafficking activities.__

According to ATF guidelines for implementing the *Gun Control Act*, the statutes that are most useful in investigating illegal firearms trafficking activities include 18 U.S.C. §§ 922 and 924.[77] These statutes include subsections that address falsifying information when purchasing a gun. Neither statute specifically prohibits firearms trafficking or straw purchasing.[78]

We analyzed ATF data on all Project Gunrunner cases referred to USAOs for prosecution between FY 2004 and FY 2009 and identified the most frequently used statutes and the average sentences given in cases that were prosecuted federally.[79] ATF used 75 different statutes to obtain federal prosecutions of Project Gunrunner cases during that period.[80] We determined through our interviews of ATF personnel and analysis of ATF cases referred to USAOs for prosecution that four of the statutes are most often used to build cases against firearms traffickers:

1. Knowingly making a false statement – 18 U.S.C. § 924(a)(1)(A) – ATF commonly uses this charge for straw purchasers who knowingly made false statements to gun dealers or in the records that gun dealers are required to maintain (Form 4473);

2. Knowingly making a false statement in connection with a firearm purchase – 18 U.S.C. § 922(a)(6) – ATF commonly uses this charge when individuals make false statements that affect the legality of sales;[81]

---

[77] ATF Order 3310.4B, Firearms Enforcement Program (February 1989), 109.

[78] In fact, the term "trafficking" appears in the *Gun Control Act* only in §§ 924(c)(1), 924(g), and 929, and in those places it refers to the use of a gun during *drug* trafficking.

[79] We noted that ATF used 25 different statutes to refer Project Gunrunner cases to state prosecutors.

[80] Table 1 (in the Background section of this report) provides the top 10 statutes used for prosecution of Project Gunrunner cases during that period.

[81] The difference between 18 U.S.C. § 922(a)(6) and 18 U.S.C. § 924(a)(1)(A) pertains to whether the false statement in question affected the legality of the gun sale. Defendants can be charged with 18 U.S.C. § 922(a)(6) if, for example, they lied about their ages because they were under 18 or lied about their state residency because they were from another

Cont.

3. Knowing possession of a firearm by a convicted felon –
18 U.S.C. § 922(g)(1) – ATF uses this charge for convicted criminals who qualify as "prohibited persons" under the *Gun Control Act* and can be prosecuted for being in possession of a firearm; and

4. Willfully engaging in firearms business without a license –
18 U.S.C. § 922(a)(1)(A) – ATF commonly uses this charge when individuals deal in guns as a regular course of trade or business. Those who make occasional gun sales cannot be charged under this statute.

Statutes used to prosecute firearms traffickers carry relatively low sentences, particularly for straw purchasers of guns.

According to our analysis of ATF data, the penalties imposed for violations of the four statutes that ATF most frequently used to combat firearms trafficking with Project Gunrunner cases are lower than penalties for violations of statutes on other types of Project Gunrunner cases. The difference is especially acute when compared to penalties imposed for violations with a drug nexus. However, criminal defendants are often charged with criminal statutes that include firearms trafficking offenses and other crimes which carry longer sentences. For drug conspiracy violations, the penalties imposed average almost 10 years. In comparison, although straw purchasing is one of the most frequent methods used to divert guns out of lawful commerce according to ATF, we found defendants convicted of offenses related to only this criminal activity are generally sentenced to less than 1 year in prison. Figure 5 compares sentences of defendants convicted only under each of the statutes used in Project Gunrunner firearms trafficking cases with sentences for violations of drug-related statutes.

---

state. A defendant's false statement in a § 922(a)(6) prosecution must concern a fact material to the lawfulness of the firearms transaction. Conversely, prosecutions for 18 U.S.C. § 924(a)(1)(A) do not need to prove the defendant intended to affect the legality of the sale. Rather, this statute requires: "(1) the defendant knowingly made a false statement; and (2) the statement pertained to information that the law requires [a gun dealer] to keep."

Figure 5: Average Prison Sentences in Months for Project Gunrunner Cases by Statute, FY 2004 through FY 2009

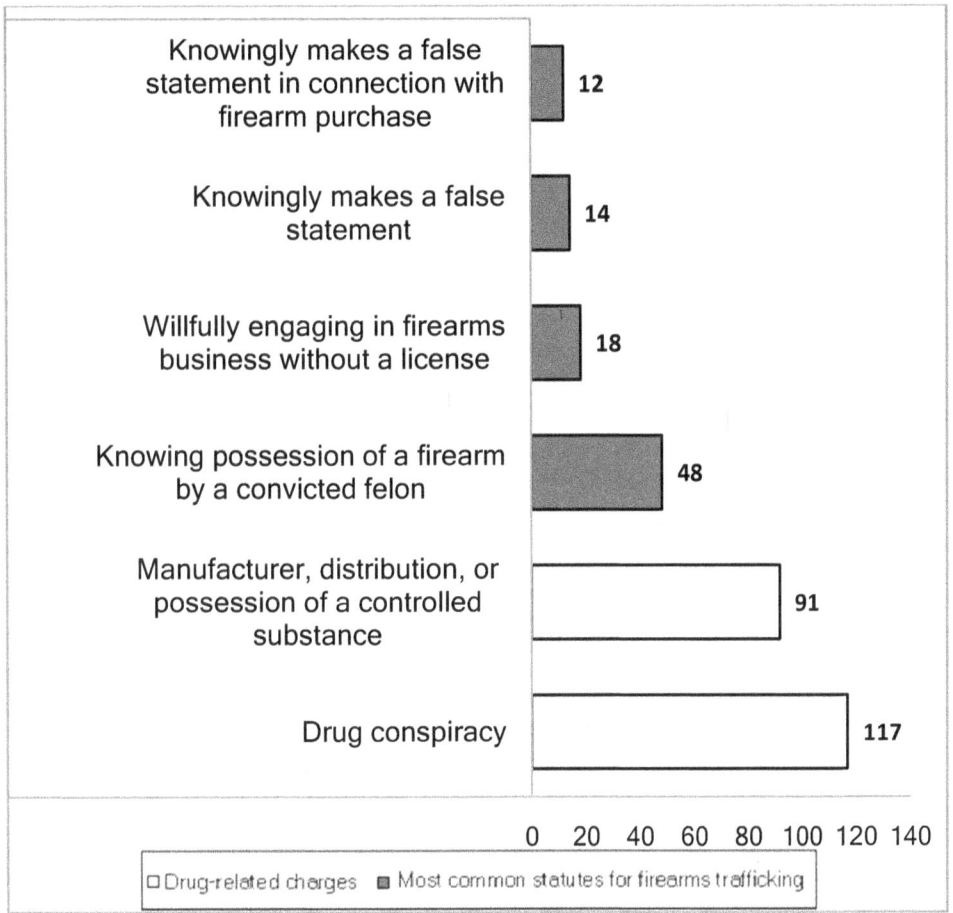

Source: OIG analysis of N-Force data.

Figure 6 shows the average prison sentences for defendants charged with sole violations of the four statutes that ATF most used on Project Gunrunner firearms trafficking cases between FY 2004 and FY 2009 compared with the maximum penalties.

Figure 6: Average Prison Sentences for Project Gunrunner Cases and Maximum Allowable Sentences, FY 2004 through FY 2009

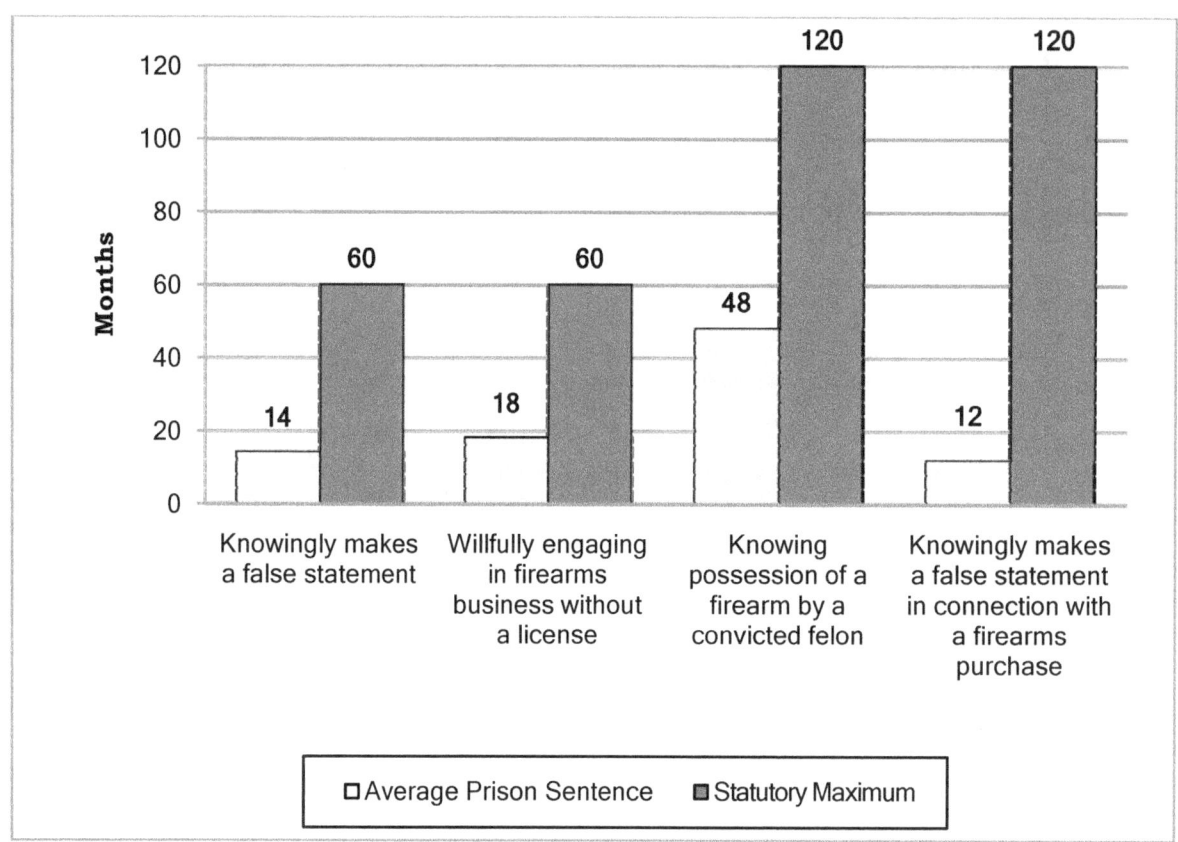

Source: OIG analysis of N-Force data.

<u>Sentencing Guidelines provide short sentences for firearms trafficking violations</u>.

We examined the Sentencing Guidelines for the statutes that ATF most frequently used in charging defendants with firearms trafficking.[82] Under the Guidelines, straw purchasing-related offenses are categorized as lesser crimes, punishable by 10 to 16 months in prison. This is because these crimes are assigned low "offense levels" and because to legally purchase a gun, by definition, a gun purchaser must have had no prior felony convictions. The OIG's analysis of ATF's case data found that 40 percent of all defendants who were charged and convicted of "knowingly

---

[82] The guidelines, established by the U.S. Sentencing Commission, "provide federal judges with fair and consistent sentencing ranges to consult at sentencing" and, among other things, are "designed to incorporate the purposes of sentencing (i.e., just punishment, deterrence, incapacitation, and rehabilitation)." U.S. Sentencing Commission, "An Overview of the United States Sentencing Commission" (June 2009), www.ussc.gov/general /USSC_Overview_200906.pdf (accessed July 2010). In *United States* v. *Booker* 375 F.3d 508 (04-104) 543 (2005), the U.S. Supreme Court ruled that binding sentencing guidelines are unconstitutional and that the guidelines were no longer binding.

making a false statement in connection with firearm purchase" (18 U.S.C. § 922(a)(6)) – one of the primary charges associated with straw purchasing – received only probation.

USAOs often decline Project Gunrunner cases that are based on the most commonly used statutes.

USAOs are less likely to accept and to prosecute ATF's Project Gunrunner cases for several reasons, including the lower penalties described above. We found that AUSAs often decline Project Gunrunner cases because they believe it is difficult to obtain convictions on the violations established in the four statutes that ATF typically uses for firearms trafficking and because they believe it is difficult to obtain evidence from Mexico. We also found that USAOs decline to prosecute ATF Project Gunrunner cases that are based on the four statutes at a much higher rate than Project Gunrunner cases citing violations of other statutes.

We examined the reasons for the declinations of Project Gunrunner cases recorded in the Executive Office for United States Attorneys' case management system, Legal Information Office Network System (LIONS).[83] Of the 125 cases recorded as declined in N-Force, there were 45 cases for which declination reasons were recorded in LIONS.[84] For those 45 cases, USAOs gave 12 different reasons for declination in LIONS. The most common reasons USAOs declined these cases were a "lack of evidence of criminal intent" or "weak or insufficient admissible evidence," accounting for a combined 38 percent (17 of 45 cases). Other reasons USAOs cited for declining Project Gunrunner cases were resource-related, such as "lack of investigative resources" or "lack of prosecutorial resources," a combined 11 percent (5 of 45). In addition, ATF agents told us that they do not refer cases to the USAOs that they assume would be rejected.

---

[83] In response to an OIG recommendation made in our review on the Department's efforts to prevent staff sexual abuse of inmates (Evaluation and Inspections Report I-2009-004), in a November 24, 2009, memorandum to all USAOs, the EOUSA Director required that all declinations of cases be entered into LIONS, whether an investigative agency presents the referral in writing and the USAO immediately declines it ("immediate declination"), or a matter is opened in LIONS and the USAO later decides to close the matter without filing charges ("later declination"). However, EOUSA officials noted that many declinations occur informally, such as over the telephone, in which case the reasons for the declination have not been recorded in LIONS in the past. In June 2010, EOUSA reported to the OIG that it was still considering revising its policy to require the recording of all declinations.

[84] As a part of this review, we did not examine the reasons for the decisions by USAOs to decline Project Gunrunner cases referred to them for prosecution by ATF.

AUSAs believe ATF's Project Gunrunner cases are difficult to prosecute.

In discussions with the OIG, Department and USAO attorneys explained that proving the elements necessary to obtain convictions under the statutes used to combat firearms trafficking is difficult. For example, a Deputy Assistant Attorney General who was a former AUSA told the OIG that willfully engaging in a firearms business without a license is a very difficult charge to prove because the government has to prove that an individual was acting in a business capacity. To do that, ATF must establish that the sale was not a private transaction but was part of a revenue earning enterprise. In practice, this means ATF must get the suspect to admit or acknowledge selling guns "willfully," as specified in the statute.[85] According to the Deputy Assistant Attorney General, many suspects can avoid prosecution simply by claiming they were selling guns from their private collection, which is not a crime.

We also found that some of the reluctance of prosecutors to accept ATF's Project Gunrunner cases appeared to be because of concerns over difficulties in obtaining evidence from Mexico. For example, building a case against a firearms trafficker may require the prosecutor to obtain evidence from Mexico to prove that the gun seized in Mexico is the same one purchased by an individual in the United States. Several AUSAs we interviewed told us that because they believed that the process for obtaining this evidence is cumbersome and time consuming, they had never attempted to obtain evidence from Mexico. In contrast, ATF personnel in Mexico City who are familiar with evidentiary matters told us that the process of obtaining this evidence was straightforward and undemanding, although underused.

Similarly, some prosecutors were unsure how to establish that a case has a nexus to gun trafficking to Mexico and were unaware that a gun trace can prove a gun acquired by a straw purchaser ended up in Mexico. This lack of understanding is important because five out of six AUSAs we spoke with told us that proving that a case has a nexus to Mexico is key to their decision to accept the case.

---

[85] 18 U.S.C. § 922(a)(1) states, "It shall be unlawful for any person except a licensed importer, licensed manufacturer, or licensed dealer, to engage in the business of importing, manufacturing, or dealing in firearms, or in the course of such business to ship, transport, or receive any firearm in interstate or foreign commerce; or except a licensed importer or licensed manufacturer, to engage in the business of importing or manufacturing ammunition, or in the course of such business, to ship, transport, or receive any ammunition in interstate or foreign commerce."

<u>AUSAs decline more ATF Project Gunrunner cases involving firearms trafficking than Project Gunrunner cases not involving firearms trafficking</u>.

We examined ATF data regarding referrals of 607 cases from FY 2004 through FY 2009 that cited at least one of the four statutes most used by ATF to charge firearms traffickers. According to ATF's case management system, 29 percent of the referrals to USAOs were pending a decision as of April 2010. Of the referrals that had been responded to by USAOs, the referrals based on the statute knowingly making a false statement in connection with a gun purchase were declined by USAOs 32 percent of the time, and those based on the statute knowingly making a false statement were declined 21 percent of the time. Referrals based on the statute willfully engaging in a firearms business without a license were declined 24 percent of the time and those based on knowing possession of a firearm by a convicted felon were declined less frequently – 12 percent of the time.

In contrast, AUSAs declined Project Gunrunner referrals that were not directly related to firearms much less frequently during FY 2004 through FY 2009. For example, when ATF pursued the statute "manufacturer, distribution, or possession of a controlled substance" (21 U.S.C. § 841(a)(1)) in a Project Gunrunner case, it was declined only 7 percent of the time and "drug conspiracy" (21 U.S.C. § 846) was declined 9 percent of the time. Significantly, the statute "use of a communication device in furtherance of drug trafficking" (21 U.S.C. § 843(b)) was never declined by federal prosecutors. We also found that USAOs responded more promptly to ATF Project Gunrunner referrals not directly related to firearms. ATF's case management system reflected that only 5 percent of the referrals that were not directly related to firearms trafficking were awaiting a response from a USAO, compared to 29 percent of firearms-related referrals.

<u>AUSAs stated they were less likely to prosecute ATF's firearms trafficking-related Project Gunrunner cases</u>.

Overall, our interviews with AUSAs in Southwest border districts indicated that the factors cited above make USAOs less likely to dedicate their resources to ATF's firearms trafficking-related Project Gunrunner cases than to other types of cases. Our interviews with AUSAs found that the lack of long sentences is also a key factor in their decisions about whether to accept these Project Gunrunner cases. As one AUSA stated, "If there were more penalties for firearms trafficking cases, you would see a lot more interest [from USAOs] in pursuing [those cases]." AUSAs told us that the limited prosecutions and low penalties reduce their ability to use the threat of prosecution to induce suspects to cooperate and provide evidence against their co-conspirators.

To improve the USAOs' support for and understanding of firearms trafficking-related Project Gunrunner cases, in June 2009 ATF's Assistant Director for Field Operations directed all ATF field divisions to meet with their respective U.S. Attorneys to convey the importance of firearms trafficking.[86] However, three AUSAs and some ATF agents told the OIG that much more communication is needed.

Some ATF agents are reluctant to refer cases because they believe the cases will not be accepted for prosecution.

In addition to the high USAO declination rate for Project Gunrunner cases focused on firearms traffickers, ATF agents told us that they do not refer many cases to the USAOs that they assume would be rejected because of criteria set by individual USAOs. For example, ATF agents told us that the USAO in one Southwest Border district will not seek to indict a suspect for willfully engaging in a firearms business without a license unless the suspect was given an official "cease and desist" letter and then was caught committing the same crime again. This burden of proof, according to ATF agents, means that many agents do not bother to present such cases to USAOs for prosecution.

Similarly, straw purchasing cases, in which a suspect obtains one or more guns on behalf of a prohibited person, were also identified by ATF as likely to be declined by USAOs. In fact, one AUSA stated that he declines straw purchasing cases because they lack "jury appeal" and result in light sentences. The Deputy Assistant Attorney General also stated that because straw purchasers' crime is essentially lying on a federal form, many judges and defense attorneys treat the crime as "paperwork violations." Consequently, agents told us, they may not even refer straw purchasing cases for prosecutorial consideration. Like AUSAs, ATF agents in Southwest border field divisions also told us that the lesser penalties and infrequent prosecution of trafficking offenses reduce their ability to use prosecution as a lever to obtain cooperation from defendants when they are arrested, which is important in investigating firearms trafficking rings.

---

[86] ATF National Firearms Trafficking Enforcement Implementation Plan (June 25, 2009).

ATF coordinates well with the DEA and CBP on firearms trafficking cases, but ATF and ICE do not consistently work together effectively on investigations of firearms trafficking to Mexico despite the memorandum of understanding these two agencies signed in 2009.

ATF coordinates well with the DEA and CBP, but ATF and ICE are not working together effectively on investigations.

ATF cites its coordination with other U.S. agencies – in particular, the DEA, CBP, and ICE – as an integral aspect of ATF's efforts to stem the flow of guns to Mexico under Project Gunrunner.[87]

ATF works well with the DEA and CBP in operations and investigations.

The DEA's counternarcotics mission parallels ATF's Project Gunrunner, as the two organizations are targeting the same organizations and often the same individuals. We found that the DEA and ATF support each other's investigations, and the DEA lends resources to ATF through multi-agency OCDETF task forces and other field operations. The CBP, in its role in securing the border into Mexico, also complements Project Gunrunner.

Regarding the DEA, OCDETF task forces provide an opportunity for ATF and the DEA to share information in building cases to the benefit of both agencies. In addition, in Mexico itself, where the DEA has approximately 100 staff in 11 different cities, the DEA assists ATF with gathering information on seized guns. The DEA Attaché to Mexico is currently allowing ATF to assign an agent to the DEA's Sensitive Investigations Unit, composed of U.S.-vetted and trained Mexican law enforcement personnel, and ATF uses the unit in gun-related investigations. ATF plans to assign one supervisor permanently to this unit.

Similarly, ATF reported that when it "develops credible information that firearms, explosives, and ammunition are approaching a border crossing, ATF provides information to CBP to support southbound

---

[87] Although ATF also seeks to coordinate, as necessary, with other federal agencies, including the FBI, the Secret Service, and the Internal Revenue Service, we limited our review to the agencies with which ATF has the most frequent contact under Project Gunrunner – the DEA, CBP, and ICE.

interdiction stops." Our interviews with ATF officials and documents they supplied provided numerous examples of this.

ATF and ICE are not collaborating effectively on investigations of firearms trafficking to Mexico.

ATF and ICE have overlapping authorities and responsibilities for investigating firearms trafficking to Mexico. ATF's Project Gunrunner and ICE's Operation Armas Cruzadas separately focus on firearms trafficking from the United States to Mexico. Project Gunrunner implements a range of ATF enforcement and regulatory activities, as discussed in this report, while Operation Armas Cruzadas targets firearms trafficking as a smuggling violation. ATF cannot effectively combat firearms trafficking to Mexico without border and smuggling enforcement by ICE, and ICE cannot always investigate smugglers without investigating the source of these guns (gun dealers and gun shows). Despite this, we found that ATF and ICE have not worked well together in their respective firearms

Memorandum of Understanding Between ATF and ICE, June 2009
• Recognizes the relevant jurisdiction of each agency and the legal authority granting each its respective jurisdiction.
• Instructs ATF and ICE to share intelligence that relates to the jurisdiction of the other agency "in a timely manner."
• Acknowledges that gun dealer inspections are within the "sole purview" of ATF and investigations concerning ports of entry and borders must be coordinated through ICE.
• States that the resolution of any interagency conflicts will begin at the lowest level possible.
• Instructs ATF and ICE that when it becomes apparent that an investigation leads into an area of concurrent jurisdiction, the agencies must "coordinate all pertinent and necessary information concerning that investigation and do so at the local level."

trafficking investigations. A memorandum of understanding (MOU) between ATF and ICE, which was updated in June 2009 to address firearms trafficking investigations and related activities, has not significantly improved coordination between the two agencies.[88]

The MOU between ATF and ICE states, "The Agencies recognize the inherent and shared responsibility to operate collaboratively in order to ensure the mutual success of the activities of both agencies . . . ." The agreement further directs the two agencies to "coordinate all pertinent and necessary information concerning firearms/explosives investigations implicating both ATF's and ICE's authorities."

---

[88] The MOU between ICE and ATF was signed by the Acting Director of ATF and the Assistant Secretary of ICE on June 30, 2009, updated from a previous version. The agreement was made in response to the GAO's report, *Firearms Trafficking: U.S. Efforts to Combat Arms Trafficking to Mexico Face Planning and Coordination Challenges,* GAO-09-709 (June 2009).

We found that some field staff do not know what the MOU requires of them, while other agents were reluctant to implement its provisions. Many ATF and ICE field personnel we interviewed misinterpreted the intent of the MOU as being to keep everyone "in their own lanes," meaning to keep ICE from conducting investigations at the source of firearms trafficking and ATF from investigations that involve smuggling, rather than "to strengthen the partnership between the agencies," as the MOU states.

One supervisor stated that he viewed the purpose of the MOU as being to keep the other agency from "screwing things up." Another supervisor, referring to one specific field office as "a loose cannon," told the OIG that if everyone would "stay in their lane, we would all work together better." Yet another supervisor told the OIG that he had no problems with the other agency precisely because those agents stay in their lanes. A different supervisor said the MOU had not changed anything, particularly in jurisdictional overlap, despite what he described as the two agencies' "mutual dependency." Another conceded to the OIG that he was unfamiliar with the contents of the MOU.

ATF and ICE field personnel described to us incidents in which one provision of the MOU, which stated that all ICE operations at gun dealers must be coordinated with ATF, was not adhered to. For example, one ATF field supervisor told us that ICE tried to assign an undercover agent to a gun dealer without coordinating with ATF. According to the ATF supervisor, the ICE agent involved said he had never read the MOU and did not realize the MOU required notification to ATF.

Another area of concern expressed by ATF personnel is ICE's criminal enforcement activities at gun shows. ICE agents reported to us that ICE's gun show operations, which began in early 2009, are a key component of ICE's Operation Armas Cruzadas. As a part of this Operation, ICE agents may act on information from an informant or other intelligence source, which may involve investigating suspicious straw purchase activity at gun shows. ATF officials cited several concerns about whether ICE had adequate justification for some of the enforcement activities it conducted at gun shows; that ICE's interaction with sellers at gun shows may be erroneously viewed by gun dealers as an ATF Industry Operations compliance inspection, which by law can occur only once a year for each gun dealer; and, that ATF's relationships with gun dealers, a primary source of ATF investigative leads, may be harmed by ICE's actions at gun shows.

ATF supervisors also expressed concern about ICE's use of eTrace. The MOU states that ICE must inform ATF when ICE initiates an investigation as the result of a gun trace. This provision of the MOU seeks to deconflict agency activities. However, ICE and ATF personnel we interviewed told us that these notifications are not always made. For example, one ICE field office supervisor stated his agents do not necessarily inform ATF when they initiate an investigation based on trace results. Our analysis of gun trace data shows that in calendar year 2009, ICE submitted 84 Mexican crime guns traced to gun dealers in that Southwest border ICE supervisor's jurisdictional area, 19 of which had a time-to-crime of less than a year. However, according to ATF field supervisors in Mexico, ICE had notified ATF of only one or two investigations it initiated based on these traces.

We also found some instances of ATF personnel not fully complying with provisions of the MOU. In one field office, ATF routinely failed to notify ICE of ongoing investigations with a direct link to the border. Additionally, an ICE field supervisor sought to assign an ICE agent to two different ATF firearms trafficking groups to foster coordination and encourage the sharing of resources and information. However, ICE personnel told us that the offer was rejected by the supervisors of both ATF firearms trafficking groups. According to the ICE supervisor, one of these ATF supervisors stated, "What can ICE do for me?" That ATF supervisor later said the same thing to the OIG.

Another ATF supervisor told us that neither agency involves the other in an investigation until the case is "firm," rather than involving the other agency early on. A senior ATF intelligence official told us, "We are in a constant struggle with ICE about stepping into each other's jurisdiction and sharing information."

Agents are not routinely sharing information and intelligence.

The number of joint firearms trafficking investigations involving ATF and ICE has increased since Project Gunrunner began. According to data from ATF's N-Force system, the number of joint investigations related to Project Gunrunner increased from 17 in FY 2005 to 53 in FY 2008, although the number dropped to 35 in FY 2009.[89] Despite the increase in joint investigations, we found that coordination problems remain. The MOU mandates that each agency is to notify the other "in a timely manner" of intelligence relating to the other's jurisdiction. That is, ICE must provide to ATF intelligence relating to a gun dealer and ATF must provide to ICE intelligence on illegal exports, including guns, crossing the U.S. border.

---

[89] On October 1, 2010, in response to a draft of this report, ICE provided the OIG with a list of 113 instances in which ICE and ATF jointly investigated between June 2009 and September 24, 2010. According to ICE, only 37 (33 percent) of these joint investigative efforts specifically addressed firearms trafficking to Mexico. Moreover, we do not believe that a list of examples of cases which ICE and ATF jointly investigated undermines the underlying findings in this section of the report. As we note, ATF initiated over 1,800 Project Gunrunner cases between FY 2007 and FY 2009, only 105 (6 percent) of which are shown to be joint investigations in ATF's case management system.

According to our interviews, this is often not occurring. For example, one ICE agent working on Operation Armas Cruzadas told the OIG that his team never receives notification about cases involving firearms trafficking to Mexico, despite several large ATF investigations in that field office. An ICE supervisor we interviewed characterized this type of notification as occurring "to a pretty limited degree," creating "a missed opportunity for [ATF]."

We also found that many of the problems between ATF and ICE personnel arise out of a lack of knowledge of the other agency's jurisdiction and operations. ATF has a well-developed specialty in firearms and explosives investigations. ATF's eTrace system and multiple sales of handgun information can provide investigative leads and intelligence of use to both agencies. ICE has a specialty in cross-border and smuggling crimes. Although ATF has always conducted firearms trafficking cases that include international trafficking, ICE agents have extensive experience in these types of cases. Some ICE agents stated that they feel they are not being used as experts on export violations and that ATF does not fully understand these types of investigations. One ICE Special Agent in Charge told us, "ATF needs to recognize that [when] anything crosses that border in either direction, we [ICE] have jurisdiction." Another ICE agent referred to a specific case in which ATF hoped to charge a suspect with smuggling violations in an upcoming trial, but ICE had to decline the case referral from ATF because the process of establishing smuggling violations takes much longer than the time ATF allotted. He opined that, had ICE been involved earlier, the smuggling case could have been developed and prosecuted.

ATF has rarely used ICE's smuggling charges against gun traffickers, which can yield longer sentences than firearm charges.

We found that despite the longer sentence prosecutors could obtain from convicting a defendant of smuggling charges, ATF has not frequently used 18 U.S.C. § 554, which makes smuggling contraband from the United States a federal offense. Although ICE has primary jurisdiction to enforce 18 U.S.C. § 554, coordination with ICE could allow ATF's Project Gunrunner defendants to be charged under this statute and could result in lengthier sentences than under the four charges most commonly used by ATF in firearms trafficking cases.

However, we found that from FY 2004 through FY 2009, only seven defendants in Project Gunrunner cases were convicted of smuggling.[90] As Figure 7 illustrates, our analysis found that the average sentence for

---

[90] Of the seven defendants in ATF cases convicted of smuggling charges, we were able to verify that six of the seven were trafficking guns to Mexico or Guatemala. In addition to "smuggling goods from the United States," these defendants were convicted of additional violations such as "willfully engaging in firearms business without a license," which added to their sentences.

smuggling violations was 5 years (60 months), several times longer than the average sentences for the types of convictions frequently made from ATF investigations.

Figure 7: Average Prison Sentences for Project Gunrunner Cases

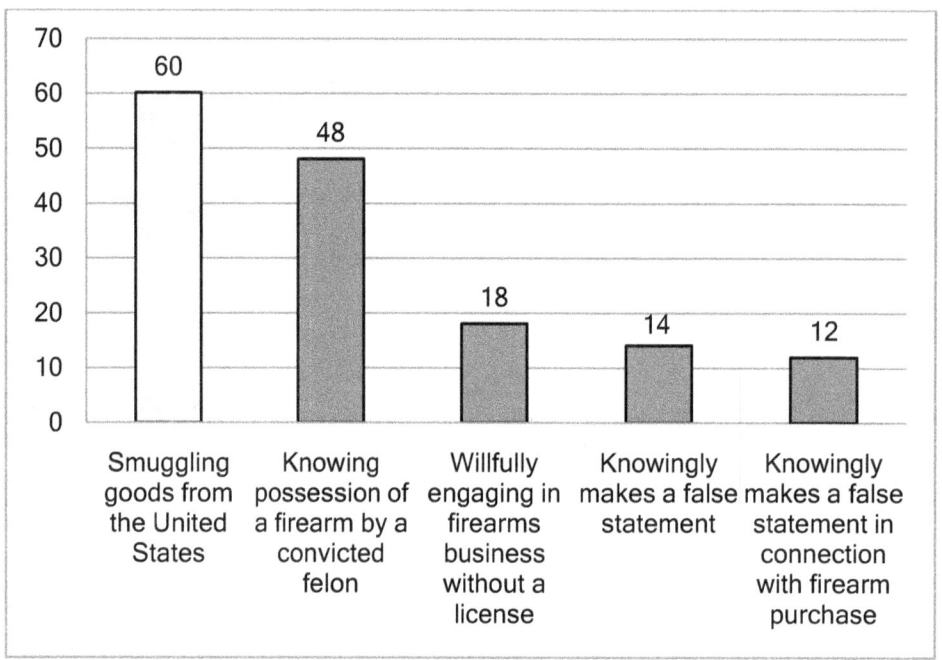

Source: OIG analysis of N-Force data.

Recommendation

We recommend that ATF:

10. Provide guidance to ATF field supervisors and agents to better coordinate with ICE, including direction on how to "coordinate all pertinent and necessary information" in areas of "concurrent jurisdiction," as defined in the memorandum of understanding.

ATF's attempts to expand gun tracing in Mexico have been unsuccessful. Although the number of trace requests from Mexico has increased since FY 2006, most seized guns in Mexico are not traced. Moreover, most trace requests from Mexico do not succeed in identifying the gun dealer who originally sold the gun, and the rate of successful traces has declined since the start of Project Gunrunner. Most Mexican crime gun trace requests that were successful were untimely and of limited use for generating investigative leads. Senior Mexican law enforcement authorities we interviewed do not view gun tracing as an important investigative tool because of limitations in the information tracing typically provides and because ATF has not adequately communicated the value of gun tracing to Mexican officials.

Despite ATF's efforts to increase the tracing of guns seized in Mexico, traces are not producing usable investigative leads.

Gun tracing can help ATF identify firearm traffickers operating in the United States and in Mexico. Gun tracing can also provide intelligence regarding patterns and trends in gun trafficking.

In its June 2007 Project Gunrunner strategy, ATF established the implementation of eTrace in Mexico and improvements in its intelligence capabilities as two of the four key operational elements of Project Gunrunner. Further, the Project Gunrunner strategy states, "In order for intelligence relating to [Project Gunrunner] to be of value, it must be 'real time' in nature."

Yet, we found that most crime guns seized in Mexico are not traced and trace requests often cannot be completed because of missing or improperly entered gun data. Further, Mexican trace requests often are not submitted on a timely basis. As a result, most Mexican crime guns that can be traced were initially sold too long ago to yield useful investigative leads.[91]

---

[91] ATF stated that its common definition of a "successful trace" is a trace that provides any additional historical or identifying information concerning the firearm beyond the original information submitted in the trace request. However, some ATF staff provided different definitions of a successful trace, such as one that identifies the first purchaser. We define a successful trace as one that identifies the gun dealer who originally sold the weapon because that is the minimum result that can provide ATF with usable intelligence

Cont.

Therefore, few investigative leads and intelligence were developed from Mexican crime gun traces.

ATF's attempts to expand tracing in Mexico have been unsuccessful.

ATF considers Mexican law enforcement's participation in tracing crime guns – by obtaining seized guns and entering the required information into eTrace – vital to the success of Project Gunrunner. Because ATF and other U.S. law enforcement agencies have no authority to conduct their own investigations in Mexico, ATF relies on Mexican officials to collect accurate crime gun information.

Under Project Gunrunner, ATF had intended to deploy a new Spanish language eTrace to all 31 state crime laboratories in Mexico to expand gun tracing. ATF reported that after its Spanish eTrace pilot program in December 2009, ATF deployed Spanish eTrace to all Spanish-language users in March 2010. However, as of June 2010, ATF Mexican federal authorities still had not agreed to deploy Spanish eTrace to the state laboratories. We asked officials from the Mexico Attorney General's office and the Secretariat of Public Security why they were unwilling to provide Mexican state police laboratories with access to Spanish eTrace. They stated that illegal possession of guns is a federal offense in Mexico and not within the jurisdiction of the Mexican states. They said all gun-related investigative and intelligence activity, including tracing, should be centralized at the national level. The officials told us that they fear decentralizing gun tracing would lead to duplication of effort between federal and state governments, an increased rate of errors by state officials who are untrained and inexperienced, and operational confusion.

ATF has continued its efforts to promote eTrace use among Mexican officials, with the ultimate goal of Mexican officials independently conducting comprehensive gun tracing. Following a September 2010 eTrace memorandum of understanding between ATF and the government of Mexico, ATF told us it plans to provide Spanish eTrace and firearms identification training to approximately 300 Mexican Attorney General staff located in Mexico City and all 31 states beginning in November 2010. ATF plans to provide eTrace user accounts to the PGR staff who received the training.

---

information. Trace requests that cannot be completed because of missing or improperly entered gun data are considered "unsuccessful traces."

<u>The number of trace requests from Mexico has increased since FY 2006, but most seized guns are not traced</u>.

Mexican crime gun trace requests to ATF have increased since Project Gunrunner was established. The number of traces of Mexican crime guns increased from 5,834 in FY 2004 to almost 22,000 in FY 2009.

Yet, in a June 2009 report, the GAO estimated that less than a quarter of crime guns transferred to the Mexican Attorney General's office in 2008 were submitted to ATF for tracing.[92] ATF Mexico Country Office staff said that CENAPI traces only weapons from high-profile seizures. Although ATF provided CENAPI with 10 laptops and trained CENAPI staff on how to submit traces through eTrace, ATF Mexico Country Office staff reported that Mexican officials are not entering many trace requests. Specifically, ATF reported that from FY 2007 through FY 2009, only about 6 percent of Mexican crime gun traces were entered into eTrace by CENAPI personnel. The remaining 94 percent of traces were entered by ATF personnel on behalf of CENAPI. Consequently, ATF Mexico Country Office personnel told us that, whenever they can, they respond to the scene of the seizures and initiate trace requests themselves on behalf of CENAPI.

However, if ATF or CENAPI does not collect tracing information quickly, it becomes unavailable. In accordance with Mexican law, all guns seized by the Mexican government must be surrendered to the Mexican military, generally within 48 hours. We determined that after the Mexican military obtains custody of the guns, ATF or CENAPI is unlikely to gain timely access to them to gather the information needed to initiate traces. Mexican military officials we interviewed said their role is to safeguard the weapons and that they have no specific authority to assist in trafficking investigations. Officially, these weapons are the property of the Mexican court.

To gain access to the weapons, ATF officials told us that they must make a formal request to the Mexico Attorney General's office for each gun, (1) citing a specific reason that access is needed, (2) demonstrating that the requested information is related to a Mexican criminal investigation, and (3) providing a description of the gun with the serial number. Yet, if ATF had the gun description and serial number, ATF officials would not need to request access to the gun. Due to these barriers, ATF and wider Department efforts to gain access to weapons in Mexican military custody have not been successful. Because many weapons are transferred to the military before basic information is collected, and many weapons for which

---

[92] U.S. Government Accountability Office, *Firearms Trafficking: U.S. Efforts to Combat Arms Trafficking to Mexico Face Planning and Coordination Challenges,* GAO-09-709 (June 2009).

information is available are not traced, the majority of seized Mexican crime guns are not traced.

Most trace requests from Mexico have not been successful, and the success rate has declined since the start of Project Gunrunner.

Deployment of eTrace is only one barrier to ATF's successful development of intelligence through tracing of Mexican crime guns. Although requests from Mexico increased from FY 2005 through FY 2009, most traces were unsuccessful. Further, the success rate of Mexican crime gun trace requests has declined since the start of Project Gunrunner. As illustrated in Figure 8, in FY 2005, 44 percent (661 of 1,518) of Mexican crime gun traces were successful. The success rate fell to 27 percent (4,059 of 14,979 in FY 2007 and remained only at 31 percent (6,664 of 21,726) in FY 2009. We found that the rate of successful traces was far lower for traces initiated in Mexico than for those initiated in the United States. By comparison, successful traces from within the vicinity of ATF's Houston Field Division ranged from 64 percent in FY 2005 to 68 percent in FY 2009.

Figure 8: Total Number of Mexican Crime Gun Traces and Number of Successful Traces, by Fiscal Year

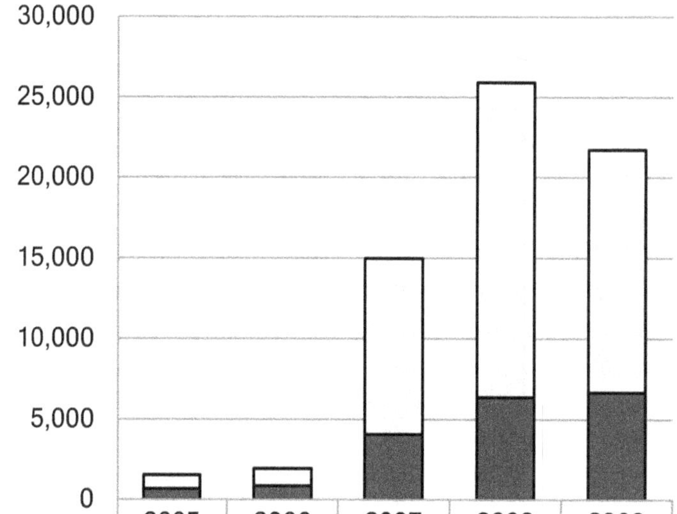

	2005	2006	2007	2008	2009
□ Number of Unsucessful Traces	857	1,063	10,920	19,541	15,062
■ Number of Successful Traces	661	841	4,059	6,360	6,664

Source: OIG analysis of ATF data.

Many of the reasons trace requests from Mexico were unsuccessful are attributable to preventable human error. According to the National Tracing Center and our own data analysis, an invalid serial number was the most common reason for unsuccessful traces from Mexico. The number of trace requests from Mexico that failed because of serial number errors more than doubled since Project Gunrunner began, increasing from 11 percent in FY 2005 to 26 percent in FY 2009. Crime gun traces can be unsuccessful for many other reasons. For example, a trace request may be unsuccessful if no manufacturer or importer is identified, if the gun predates the start of ATF's tracing program in 1969, or if the necessary gun dealer records are not obtainable. ATF staff in Mexico City told the OIG that they had noted these types of errors on incoming requests and that these errors could be prevented through training Mexican law enforcement personnel.

However, we found that the training of Mexican law enforcement in firearms identification has not resulted in accurate trace submissions by Mexican law enforcement. ATF reported that between calendar years 2007 and 2009, it had trained 961 Mexican law enforcement personnel in firearms identification and tracing. In discussions with the OIG, ATF and Mexican authorities stated that further training is needed. The poor quality of the tracing data and the resulting high rate of unsuccessful traces suggest that either the training is insufficient, training has been provided to the wrong people, or there are other unidentified problems with Mexican law enforcement's crime gun tracing.

Most successful Mexican crime gun trace requests were nonetheless untimely and of limited use for generating investigative leads.

Many ATF field and intelligence personnel told us that trace information they received from successful traces on Mexican crime guns was of limited use because the time-to-crime interval was too long.[93] According to ATF staff, many successful traces of Mexican crime guns are not worth acting upon because few federal prosecutors will accept cases with a time-to-crime of over 3 years, and some will not accept a case with a time-to-crime of over a year.[94] The large majority of crime guns that are

---

[93] ATF defines time-to-crime as "the period of time (measured in days) between a gun's acquisition from a retail market and law enforcement's recovery of that gun during use, or suspected use, in a crime." See ATF Order 3310.4B, Firearms Enforcement Program (February 1989), 110. However, the time-to-crime data for Mexican crime guns is not always based on the actual recovery date because, according to ATF personnel, when a recovery date is unknown, ATF uses the trace request date to calculate the time-to-crime. ATF personnel also said time-to-crime statistics for Mexican crime guns are skewed because of a large amount of crime gun data the government of Mexico provided to ATF in 2009 regarding guns seized years before.

[94] The statute of limitations for straw purchasing-related crimes is 5 years. See 18 U.S.C. § 3282. Notwithstanding the 5-year statute of limitations, we found that many Southwest border USAOs establish much shorter thresholds for the prosecution of these types of cases. For example, the Northern District of Texas (encompassing ATF's Dallas Field Division) typically will not accept ATF straw purchasing-related cases with a time-to-

Cont.

recovered in Mexico and traced – over 75 percent – have a time-to-crime of over 5 years. Only 18.2 percent of recovered crime guns have a time-to-crime of less than 3 years. Further, the long time-to-crime interval has been exacerbated because ATF has been unable to gain timely access to the guns seized by Mexican law enforcement.

ATF officials told us that some gun trace requests submitted to ATF by Mexican officials in 2009 were of guns that had been held in Mexican federal storage for 3 years or longer prior to being submitted for tracing. In one particularly large volume trace request from Mexican officials to ATF, very few of the guns had been seized by Mexican law enforcement within the year previous to the submission of the trace request. Consequently, this information provided to ATF was of limited use for identifying ongoing trafficking conspiracies.

<u>Mexican law enforcement authorities do not view gun tracing as an important investigative tool</u>.

We examined why Mexican law enforcement authorities do not consistently submit guns for tracing or delay their submissions. In interviews with us, Mexican law enforcement officials indicated a lack of interest in tracing. One Mexican official stated that U.S. officials talk of eTrace as if it is a "panacea" but that it does nothing for Mexican law enforcement. An official in the Mexico Attorney General's office told us he felt eTrace is "some kind of bad joke."

Mexican officials told us that they are not satisfied with the details of the information they receive on U.S. citizens and gun dealers from crime gun trace requests they submit to ATF. The officials cited this as a reason why they do not believe eTrace has benefit for Mexican law enforcement. However, we found that the information that Mexican officials are seeking extends beyond the information provided in trace results. [95] We asked Department attorneys about the legal restrictions on ATF for sharing investigative information about suspected firearms traffickers with the government of Mexico. The attorneys stated that ATF may provide Mexican law enforcement with most of the information that is returned in a typical response to an eTrace request generated by Mexican officials. It is the criminal history of suspected firearms traffickers that Mexican law enforcement is seeking which is not a part of this typical eTrace response.

---

crime of more than 1 year, while the Southern District of Texas (encompassing the Houston Field Division) established a threshold of less than 3 years for these cases.

[95] There is a memorandum of understanding between ATF and the Mexico Attorney General's office (including the office's intelligence unit, CENAPI) governing Mexico's use of eTrace. The MOU does not state that Mexican eTrace users are to be provided any less information than would U.S. law enforcement eTrace users.

However, if an investigation results in an arrest, ATF will provide information regarding the arrestee in response to an official request from Mexico.

ATF officials asserted that providing Mexican law enforcement agencies with information on U.S. purchasers and gun dealers would be of little use to Mexican authorities, whom cannot conduct investigations in the United States. Rather, it is ATF's responsibility to pursue crime gun trace leads in the United States. ATF noted that firearms tracing is not designed to "pinpoint the date, time, and place a firearm" crossed the border. ATF further noted that even if additional, detailed information might contribute to an investigation in Mexico, it would be unlikely to result in a prosecution there, as less than 3 percent of Mexican investigations are brought to trial.

We found that Mexican officials' perception is that ATF does not reciprocate information sharing with them. This remains an impediment to reciprocity in coordination between ATF and Mexican law enforcement.

Several ATF officials told us they are aware of the Mexican officials' concerns and acknowledged that ATF has not adequately communicated the value of tracing in generating leads from Mexican crime guns that can ultimately serve to reduce firearms trafficking into Mexico and its associated violence. For example, one ATF Special Agent in Charge stated, "Those guys want to know what [the] information they are providing is doing, they want to see results and I don't think we [ATF] are doing that." Another Southwest border Special Agent in Charge told us, "One of the things we [ATF] do not do well is take credit for what we do. The Mexicans say 'Ok, you want us to trace your guns, but the guns are already here. So what is it that tracing does for us?' We need to show them through training and success. We don't do that well in ATF."

We concluded that because ATF has not been able to communicate the value of gun tracing to Mexican law enforcement officials, they are less likely to prioritize their efforts to obtain tracing information from seized crime guns and enter it into eTrace. This hinders ATF's plans to deploy Spanish eTrace throughout Mexico. Because the expansion of tracing in Mexico is the "cornerstone" of Project Gunrunner, this presents a significant barrier to the successful implementation of ATF's Gunrunner strategy.

Recommendations

To gain better cooperation of Mexican law enforcement in tracing, and to increase the timeliness of trace submissions from Mexico, we recommend that ATF:

11. Work with the government of Mexico to determine the causes of unsuccessful traces and develop actions to improve the rate of successful traces.
12. Regularly and more effectively communicate ATF's Project Gunrunner strategy to Mexican law enforcement authorities, including the value of gun tracing and the successes involving information or tracing information provided by Mexican agencies.

PART VI: ATF CHALLENGES IN COORDINATING IN MEXICO

ATF has been unable to respond to many training and support requests from Mexican government agencies, and ATF's backlog of requests for information from Mexican authorities has hindered coordination between ATF and Mexican law enforcement. In addition, ATF has not staffed or structured its Mexico Country Office to fully implement Project Gunrunner's missions in Mexico. ATF faces challenges in coordinating with Mexican law enforcement authorities. There is no straightforward mechanism to facilitate the exchange of law enforcement information between ATF and a comparable Mexican law enforcement agency. Finally, ATF has not integrated the Project Gunrunner activities of its Southwest Border field divisions and its Mexico Country Office in a coordinated approach to reduce firearms trafficking from the United States to Mexico.

ATF has been unable to fully meet Mexican government requests for support under Project Gunrunner.

ATF's Mexico Country Office is unable to fully meet the workload associated with coordinating with Mexico due in part to a lack of resources. Training in firearms trafficking enables Mexican law enforcement agencies to become more effective partners for ATF, but ATF has been unable to respond to many key requests for training. Assigning ATF personnel to work directly with Mexican law enforcement is another way to enhance coordination, but ATF has not been able to assign such staff for this purpose. Additionally, we found that official requests to ATF from the government of Mexico for information on gun traffickers are backlogged at ATF's Mexico Country Office.

<u>ATF is not able to respond to many training requests from Mexico.</u>

ATF has provided training to help build Mexico's capacity to conduct its own operations to reduce firearms trafficking. In addition to the 961 Mexican law enforcement personnel that ATF trained in firearms identification and tracing between calendar years 2007 and 2009, ATF also trained 337 Mexican law enforcement personnel in firearms trafficking investigations. However, Mexican officials have sought additional training that ATF has not been able to provide. The Department of State's Narcotics Affairs Section, which facilitates funding for ATF to train Mexican law enforcement, has funded this training. However, although the Department of State has access to funds to enable the training of Mexican law enforcement, ATF has lacked the staff to provide additional requested training on basic firearms investigations, weapons handling, and firearms identification. For example, ATF has not been able to provide training at the new Secretariat of Public Security Academy, a commitment ATF made as a part of a wider Department plan to assist in training newly hired Mexican law enforcement officers. ATF had planned to teach, at a minimum, interrogation techniques there. Similarly, ATF has had to deny requests from Mexican state and local law enforcement for training in weapons handling and firearms identification and to deny CENAPI intelligence analysts training in analytical intelligence techniques.

Mexican law enforcement officials said they were disappointed that ATF has not provided more training, although officials we interviewed were appreciative of the training they have received so far. The Chief of CENAPI said that more training is needed to develop institutional knowledge that can be passed onto newer staff. A senior official from the Mexico Attorney General's office told us that the increased efforts in Mexican firearms investigations meant that the corresponding training from ATF must be expanded, noting specifically the need for firearms investigation and intelligence training. We concluded that ATF's inability to respond to training requests has hindered the development of better Mexican law enforcement capabilities that would support the goals of Project Gunrunner.

ATF's backlog of requests from Mexican authorities for information impedes coordination between ATF and Mexican law enforcement.

ATF's coordination with Mexican law enforcement is complicated by the differences between the U.S. and Mexican legal systems. The Mutual Legal Assistance Treaty with Mexico governs criminal justice interaction between the two countries.[96] The treaty mandates that except in urgent cases and in informal exchanges, requests for assistance should take place in writing and include certain information, such as the purpose for which the evidence, information, or other assistance is sought. The Mutual Legal Assistance Treaty states that both countries should "promptly comply with the requests or, when appropriate, shall transmit them to other competent authorities to do so."

In accordance with Article 4 of the treaty, Mexican law enforcement officials send such requests in official communications called *officios* to ATF in Spanish, thus requiring translation before ATF can take action. Some of the most common requests in *officios* are criminal histories on gun purchasers and detainees, and information from ATF interviews on

---

[96] Treaty on Cooperation Between the United States of America and the United Mexican States for Mutual Legal Assistance, Article 2, December 1987.

individuals linked to a multiple handgun sale in the United States. Mexican officials can use this information to generate an investigation in Mexico. ATF must translate the reply into Spanish (the language of the requesting government) before sending the information back to the requester.

ATF has a backlog of *officios* that is hindering Mexico's ability to conduct criminal cases and is affecting the relationship between ATF and Mexican law enforcement. As of June 2010, Mexico Country Office staff told us that about 200 outstanding *officios* from Mexico are awaiting responses, with 15 to 20 arriving every week. A Mexico Country Office official estimated that even if no more *officios* were to arrive, it would still take staff members assigned to that duty several months to process the current backlog.

In their discussions with us, Mexican law enforcement officials noted the impact of these delays. Of particular concern to them was that Mexican authorities would arrest suspects and send an *officio* to ATF for needed information, but by the time ATF responded the Mexican authorities had released the suspect due to lack of evidence. In addition, the lack of timely support in this area made Mexican law enforcement officials question ATF's commitment to Project Gunrunner and to ATF's Mexican law enforcement partners.

ATF has not been able to assign personnel to work alongside Mexican law enforcement.

ATF has not been able to assign personnel to work directly with Mexican law enforcement agencies, as it planned. In its 2010 Operations Plan, ATF's Mexico Country Office stated that it planned to embed ATF personnel with their Mexican counterparts, including assigning an intelligence analyst with CENAPI, one agent at the Secretariat of Public Security's headquarters, one agent in the Mexico Attorney General's office's headquarters, and an ATF supervisor with the DEA's Sensitive Investigations Unit.[97] ATF staff told us that embedding ATF personnel with Mexican law enforcement is the best way to facilitate coordination and enable Mexican law enforcement to conduct firearms trafficking investigations. This method of coordination also has the full support of Mexican law enforcement. The head of CENAPI, for example, told us he supported the idea of embedding ATF personnel because he felt this would help train his staff in firearms trafficking investigations to make his agency more effective and would help facilitate the exchange of information.

---

[97] The DEA's Sensitive Investigations Unit is the vetted unit of Mexican law enforcement officers overseen by the DEA.

However, as of June 2010, ATF has not yet been able to deploy any of these personnel. ATF personnel in Mexico City also said they have been unable to participate in several joint meetings, trainings, and exercises with the Secretariat of Public Security, Mexico Attorney General's office, and other Mexican law enforcement agencies because of the lack of available staff.

One example of the impact of ATF's inability to embed its staff with Mexican law enforcement is the temporary deactivation of the Combined Explosives Investigation Team, an ATF-initiated U.S.-Mexican group composed of staff from the Mexican military, the Mexico Attorney General's office, Secretariat of Public Security, and an ATF Certified Explosive Specialist and Explosives Enforcement Officer.[98] This unit works throughout Mexico responding to scenes where explosives were seized. According to ATF and Mexican officials, this unit is highly regarded not only by other ATF staff, but also by other U.S. law enforcement authorities and especially Mexican law enforcement authorities. Beyond the individual successes of the program, ATF staff who participated in the group told us that they were able to work alongside their Mexican counterparts, which enhanced ATF's relationships with Mexican law enforcement. Despite the successes of the unit and the progress it made in enhancing ATF's relationship with Mexican law enforcement officials, ATF Assistant Attachés told us the group was deactivated in December 2009 over the objection of Mexican law enforcement because the ATF Explosives Enforcement Officer and Certified Explosive Specialist transferred out of Mexico. In March 2010, ATF reactivated the team with newly assigned staff, augmented by Mexican personnel.

ATF is unable to recruit sufficient qualified staff to fill positions in Mexico.

ATF has experienced difficulties in recruiting qualified staff for its Mexico Country Office, which hinders ATF's ability to execute its already challenging duties in Mexico. Given the small number of Spanish-speaking employees throughout ATF, the fact that moving to Mexico is often a hardship for staff and their families, and the lack of incentives for staff to take this assignment, ATF has had difficulty attracting candidates for the positions in Mexico. ATF officials reiterated that it does not have sufficient number of Spanish-speaking agents to mandate Spanish language ability for positions in Mexico. With the escalation of cartel-related violence and the emphasis of Project Gunrunner, the need for ATF staff in Mexico has risen (Figure 9). The number of staff as of June 2010 was more than four

---

[98] Certified Explosives Specialists are ATF agents who investigate violations of federal explosives laws. Explosives Enforcement Officers specialize in explosives and bomb disposal, provide explosives device determinations for criminal prosecutions, and conduct explosives threat assessments of vulnerable buildings, airports, and national monuments.

times what it was before Project Gunrunner in 2007, and ATF has plans to assign more staff to Mexico.

Figure 9: ATF Permanent Staff Assigned in Mexico, FY 2001 through 2010

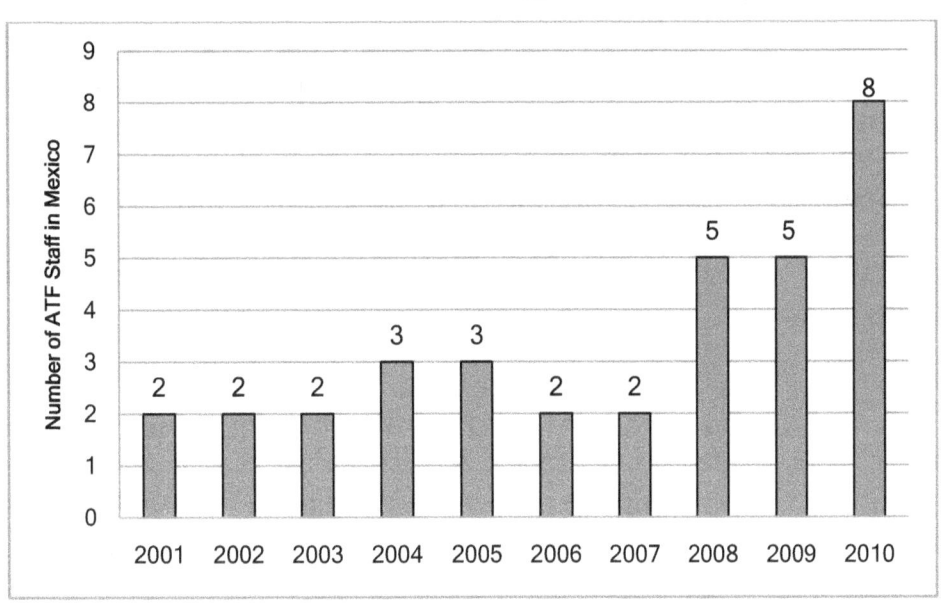

Note: Number of permanent staff at the end of each fiscal year (as of June 2010).

Source: ATF International Affairs Office.

Yet, in response to recruiting difficulties, ATF has been relying on temporary duty (TDY) personnel in Mexico rather than permanent staff. As of June 2010, ATF had 13 permanent or TDY staff assigned in Mexico, of which 5 were on TDY status. ATF permanent staff in the Mexico Country Office told the OIG that although they appreciated the assistance of the TDY staff, permanent staff were more effective because they would be in Mexico long enough to build effective relationships with Mexican counterparts and learn the culture. The ATF staff in the Mexico Country Office also said that it takes time for personnel to adjust and settle into living in Mexico, and the cost of sending TDY staff to Mexico is much higher than that of a permanent posting.

Building working relationships with Mexican law enforcement and government officials is important to the success of Project Gunrunner. When ATF personnel are assigned to Mexico for less than a year, it makes building effective relationships very difficult. The impact of the lack of stability of ATF permanent staff in Mexico is compounded by the often high turnover rate of Mexican law enforcement personnel. As an anti-corruption measure, many Mexican law enforcement positions rotate personnel frequently, as often as every 6 months. ATF officials told us this also affects their relationship with Mexican law enforcement.

ATF staff in Mexico that we interviewed suggested several incentives that would encourage qualified ATF staff to come to Mexico. They suggested, for example, reclassifying the positions in Mexico. ATF Assistant Attachés in Mexico City are GS-14s. In the United States, a GS-14 ATF agent is a supervisor of an enforcement group (Group Supervisor or Resident Agent in Charge). In ATF, serving as a supervisor is required for promotion to the GS-15 level. However, assignment as a GS-14 Assistant Attaché in Mexico does not count as a supervisory position. One Assistant Attaché in Mexico cited this as being the primary reason he had decided to transfer back to the United States. Similarly, time spent in Mexico does not count as "headquarters time," which also helps in advancing within ATF, according to agents we interviewed. ATF agents suggested that Mexico assignments should count as a supervisory assignment or a headquarters assignment, or both.

In response to a draft of this report, in September 2010 ATF reported that all permanent positions in Mexico receive "headquarters credit" for their tour of duty in Mexico. Further, ATF reported that it will upgrade the Attaché position to the Senior Executive Service level to provide that position with greater influence in interactions within ATF, and with U.S. Embassy staff and the government of Mexico.

Bonuses are another incentive that could help attract staff to Mexico. Currently, DEA and FBI personnel qualify for, and receive, "Danger Pay," which provides increased compensation when assigned to one of several cities in Mexico and other locations throughout the world.[99] This incentive is also used by the Department of State and other government agencies with staff in areas eligible for Danger Pay. However, at the time of our site visit to Mexico City in March 2010, ATF staff in Mexico were not receiving Danger Pay.

In response to a draft of this report, ATF informed us that in March 2010, the U.S. Department of State authorized Danger Pay of 15 percent for ATF staff assigned to Monterrey, Tijuana, and Ciudad Juarez. ATF reported that staff in those locations began receiving the pay effective March 14, 2010. Additionally, ATF reported that, as an incentive, all ATF staff assigned to Mexico began receiving "Difficult to Staff Incentive Pay" of 15 percent in December 2009.

Also, ATF staff in Mexico noted that the current 3-year tour of duty in Mexico is an onerous obligation. The potential of violence in Mexico creates

---

[99] According to the U.S. Department of State, Danger Pay is additional compensation above basic compensation for service at designated Danger Pay posts where civil insurrection, terrorism, or war conditions threaten physical harm or imminent danger to all U.S. government civilian employees.

a higher burden on ATF personnel and their families than other posts. ATF and Department officials told us that other federal agencies often send staff on 2-year tours, which can be extended a year.

<u>ATF's Mexico Country Office requires stronger intelligence collection, analysis, and dissemination capabilities</u>.

ATF's Mexico Country Office does not currently have the capability to collect, analyze, and disseminate all available intelligence from weapons seizures occurring in Mexico. ATF personnel in the Mexico Country Office focus their efforts on responding directly to seizure incidents in Mexico, collecting crime gun information in conjunction with Mexican officials, initiating traces, and receiving intelligence on suspected traffickers from Mexican law enforcement. According to ATF officials, there are usually about 120 to 150 gun seizures in Mexico per month. However, the small staff in ATF's Mexico Country Office is unable to respond to all seizures and keep up with the analysis of intelligence and information.

ATF's process of collecting and analyzing information on weapons seizures in Mexico is insufficient to develop intelligence to support firearms trafficking investigations. When Mexico Country Office personnel receive firearms seizure data from Mexican officials, the staff enters the data into eTrace. Office staff attempts to enhance this intelligence with additional information from Mexican law enforcement. However, this effort is limited to ATF staff because the Foreign Service Nationals assigned to the Mexico Country Office are not authorized to access ATF databases and therefore have limited ability to assist with analyzing intelligence for dissemination within ATF. Consequently, Office staff cannot collect information on many firearms seizures in Mexico. ATF representatives at EPIC also collect Mexican crime gun information from open sources such as Mexican newspapers and reports. Office of Strategic Intelligence and Information's Southwest Border Field Intelligence Support Team links EPIC's information with additional intelligence and, when appropriate, sends the intelligence to agents in the field as investigative leads. However, information collected by EPIC often duplicates information already known by the Mexico Country Office.

In its Operations Plan for 2010, the ATF Mexico Country Office identified a strategic goal to improve coordination, communication, and information sharing on firearms seizures between U.S. and Mexican agencies. To meet this goal, the Operations Plan identified a requirement to assign a new, full-time ATF analyst to work with the Mexico City Intelligence Community Group, a multi-agency intelligence group located at the U.S. Embassy in Mexico City. Although the DEA has full-time representation in this group, no one from ATF's Mexico Country Office participates as a full-time member of the group. We believe that the development of better intelligence and information collection, analysis, and dissemination capability at the Mexico Country Office would respond directly to information sharing concerns expressed to us by officials in Mexico.

ATF faces difficulty in coordinating with Mexican law enforcement officials to implement Project Gunrunner.

Despite ATF's efforts with Project Gunrunner, lack of coordination within the government of Mexico is hindering the success of Project Gunrunner. However, we found that a pilot program of assigning a Mexico Attorney General's office representative to the Phoenix Field Division has helped communication and information sharing between ATF and Mexican officials.

Mexican officials are not well informed about Project Gunrunner.

We found that senior Mexican law enforcement officials were often not fully aware of Project Gunrunner's goals, the results it has achieved, and how the program can help reduce firearms trafficking into Mexico. For example, some Mexican officials we interviewed were not aware of Project Gunrunner's successes or of the databases and information systems used to support the project. One Mexican official asked the OIG, "What is it [Project Gunrunner] exactly? Is eTrace part of it?" He complained that Project Gunrunner is a term used as a "political reference point" but that he "cannot see the effects of it." ATF officials agreed that ATF is having problems communicating its strategy and success stories to Mexican law enforcement officials. The ATF Attaché in Mexico City noted the challenge in measuring the impact of Project Gunrunner and that it is impossible to quantify the number of guns that ATF prevented from entering Mexico as a result of enforcement and regulatory programs. Other ATF officials acknowledged that ATF has not adequately communicated about Project Gunrunner with Mexican law enforcement officials. One Southwest border Special Agent in Charge said, "I don't think they [Mexican law enforcement] really understand what we do." He stated:

> We as an agency have failed to show them our success stories. 'For the information you gave, this is what it has actually resulted in.' . . . I think if we did a better job on our part, it would help. Those guys want to know what that information they are providing is doing, they want to see results, and I don't think we [ATF] are doing that. . . . They would show some gratification and satisfaction and say, 'Hey, that worked. We stopped this guy from running guns.'

U.S. officials we interviewed also referred to problems in coordination among the various Mexican law enforcement agencies responsible for combating firearms trafficking. U.S. officials described being asked to serve as intermediaries and to mediate disputes between Mexican agencies. Because there is no equivalent to ATF in Mexico (a federal agency with jurisdiction over firearms crimes), several different Mexican law enforcement agencies work on these crimes, including the Mexico Attorney General's office, its intelligence branch CENAPI, the Mexican military, and the Secretariat of Public Security. While noting that the lack of coordination among Mexican law enforcement continues to be a problem, U.S. officials also told us that there recently has been significant progress in getting Mexican law enforcement agencies to work together, especially at meetings like GC Armas.

We found that that the monthly U.S.-Mexican GC Armas meetings have to some extent improved information sharing between ATF and the government of Mexico. The meetings are intended to coordinate joint U.S.-Mexico operations related to the detection, monitoring, and detention of firearms trafficking suspects crossing the border. According to U.S. and Mexican law enforcement officials, the meetings have become an important tool for agencies to share information. At the meetings, agency representatives discuss their ongoing investigations and significant events. They also frequently make requests and discuss planning for training and intelligence needs. The Mexico Attorney General's office also provides ATF with a report of gun seizure information to be entered into eTrace.

According to officials from the Department of State and ATF, although there are problems with trust, and reservations about sharing information, the U.S.-Mexican GC Armas meetings are developing into an effective venue for sharing intelligence and information.

Information sharing between Mexican law enforcement and ATF could be improved by embedding a Mexico Attorney General's representative in each of the ATF's Southwest border field divisions.

Beyond the ad hoc relationships formed by border liaisons, the Mexico Country Office's reliance on the formal *officios* process, or information obtained from GC Armas meetings, ATF does not have a direct way to gain information from Mexican law enforcement on firearms trafficking suspects. However, in a pilot program in the Phoenix Field Division, a representative from the Mexico Attorney General's office is assigned to that division. This representative is a bilingual prosecutor who works for the Mexico Attorney General's office's intelligence branch, CENAPI, and has experience in firearms trafficking cases. He primarily responds to requests from the Phoenix Field Division by querying Mexican databases on information about suspects and other leads. He also educates ATF personnel on Mexican law enforcement and educates Mexican law enforcement personnel on ATF.

The representative told us, however, that he has been frustrated that ATF has not been able to reciprocate the information sharing. Like his counterparts in Mexico's statements to us, the representative also cited the need for more detailed information on suspected firearms traffickers who are U.S. citizens. In July 2010, ATF headquarters staff told us that ATF is drafting a Foreign Operations order that will address information sharing protocols with the government of Mexico.

According to the Phoenix Special Agent in Charge, the Mexico Attorney General's office representative has shown "the benefit to each country of being able to have someone who will positively impact the illegal flow of guns to Mexico." One example that staff from the Phoenix Field Division provided was proving the nexus of cases to Mexico, either through sharing seizure information or information on a suspect in Mexico. According to an Assistant Special Agent in Charge in Phoenix, this has made the USAO more likely to accept cases that have such a nexus. The representative also can provide information on interviews of suspects in Mexico and other personal information such as criminal history and known associates.

The Phoenix Assistant Special Agent in Charge said he endorsed the idea of having a Mexico Attorney General's office representative in each of ATF's Southwest border field divisions. A senior official from that agency agreed the arrangement is beneficial and supported sending additional representatives.

ATF has not integrated the Project Gunrunner activities of its four Southwest border field divisions and its Mexico Country Office in a coordinated approach.

To assess Project Gunrunner's overall strategy, we reviewed ATF's June 2007 Gunrunner strategy, its 2009 National Firearms Trafficking Enforcement Strategy and Implementation Plan, the 2009 firearms trafficking implementation plans of ATF's Southwest border field divisions, and ATF's Mexico Country Office 2010 Operations Plan.[100] We found that

---

[100] We reviewed the Phoenix, Dallas, and Los Angeles Field Divisions' implementation plans. The Houston Field Division did not provide any implementation plan, as of July 2010. The Mexico Country Office is not considered a field division and, accordingly, did not publish a firearms trafficking implementation plan. Rather, the Office published a separate 2010 Operations Plan which addresses its role as a country team

Cont.

these strategies and plans do not effectively address U.S.-Mexico coordination, joint operations and activities, or intelligence sharing between the field divisions and the Mexico Country Office. We believe this lack of coordinated planning has contributed to various weaknesses in Project Gunrunner, including unclear roles for border liaison personnel, inadequate and disparate staffing in the Mexico Country Office, failure to focus on complex conspiracy firearms trafficking investigations, and poor coordination with U.S. and Mexican law enforcement agencies on both sides of the border.

For example, ATF's June 2007 Gunrunner strategy specifically identified the need for a Project Gunrunner strategy that would unite the efforts of the four Southwest border field divisions and the Mexico Country Office to "affect firearms and ammunition trafficking to Mexican-based criminal organizations in both the U.S. and Mexico" and to "coordinate intelligence and information-sharing packages with the Mexico Country Office." However, none of the plans that ATF provided to us fulfilled this requirement, or explained how the Southwest border divisions and the Mexico Country Office would work together.

We found that Special Agents in Charge of the Southwest border field divisions we visited did develop internal plans to guide their respective Project Gunrunner regulatory and enforcement activities in their field divisions. However, these plans did not address coordination with the ATF Mexico Country Office. That Office is only briefly mentioned in one Southwest border division's firearms trafficking implementation plans and the plan does not specify how or under what circumstances division staff are to coordinate with the Office. Additionally, although the Mexico Country Office's 2010 Operations Plan states that the Office will assist in the interdiction of illegal arms being trafficked to Mexico, the plan makes no reference to Project Gunrunner.[101]

Further, the majority (20 of 33) of the Southwest border field division agents, intelligence personnel, and supervisors we interviewed told us they had never heard of ATF's 2009 National Firearms Trafficking Enforcement Strategy and Implementation Plan, or that they had heard of the Strategy or Plan but believed they had no impact. Staff of the ATF's Mexico Country Office also expressed concerns about ATF's lack of an integrated strategy and stated that the Southwest border field divisions communicated poorly with them and each other. One Mexico Country Office official we

---

member at the U.S. Embassy. ATF Mexico Country Office Operations Plan for 2010, "Benefits to Mission" (undated).

[101] Appendix IV provides an overview of the implementations plans provided us by ATF's Phoenix, Dallas, and Los Angeles field divisions.

---

interviewed stated, "ATF has no strategy . . . . The Southwest border field divisions don't talk to each other. There is no exchange of information. Right now, the system [to exchange information] is broken."

ATF has drafted a new strategy relating to Project Gunrunner.

In September 2010, after we provided ATF with a draft of this report, ATF issued a revised strategy for combating firearms trafficking to Mexico and related violence. ATF's new strategy included 13 key elements of a revised approach to combating cartels, such as closer coordination with other law enforcement agencies, particularly related to intelligence on drug cartels; the need to improve intelligence collection, sharing, and analysis and the prioritization of leads; improved coordination with Southwest border field divisions and the Mexico Country Office, including the use of Border Liaison Officers; focusing investigations on complex conspiracy cases and entire trafficking rings; greater use of the OCDETF Program; and improved investigative coordination and intelligence sharing with Mexican law enforcement, including on gun tracing.

ATF's strategy document recognizes the need to address many of the shortfalls we found in our review. However, the strategy document does not provide detailed information on how ATF will implement and monitor efforts to improve operations in the key areas it identified. We believe ATF's development of an implementation plan – with defined goals, specific actions, and resources – is essential to the successful implementation of improvements discussed in the September 2010 cartel strategy and also to ATF's overall effort to combat firearms trafficking to Mexico.

Recommendations

We recommend that ATF:

13. Develop better information sharing and intelligence analysis capability at its Mexico Country Office.

14. In coordination with the Mexico Attorney General's office, evaluate the mutual benefits, roles, and information sharing protocols of the Mexico Attorney General's office representative pilot program to determine whether to expand the program to each of ATF's Southwest border field divisions.

15. Ensure that the reforms discussed in ATF's September 2010 document entitled "Project Gunrunner – A Cartel Focused Strategy" are fully and expeditiously implemented.

CONCLUSION AND RECOMMENDATIONS

In implementing Project Gunrunner, ATF has increased several of its key investigative and inspection program activities, such as the numbers of cases referred for prosecution involving firearms trafficking to Mexico that is fueling deadly violence along the Southwest border, traces of firearms from Mexico, and gun dealer compliance inspections along the Southwest Border.

However, we found significant weaknesses in ATF's implementation of Project Gunrunner that undermine its effectiveness.

ATF does not use intelligence effectively to identify and target firearms trafficking organizations on both sides of the border. ATF could improve in four intelligence-related areas.

For example, we concluded that ATF needs to better coordinate and share strategic intelligence with the government of Mexico and with its U.S. law enforcement partners. In this effort, ATF should develop processes to systematically exchange timely and relevant intelligence with these agencies on both sides of the border.

ATF also needs to improve its own internal processes for collecting, analyzing and disseminating intelligence sent to field agents. ATF Field Intelligence Groups should work with their respective Southwest border enforcement groups to develop guidelines for the production of timely and relevant investigative leads. ATF managers need an automated system to track, monitor the outcome of, and evaluate the usefulness of, investigative leads.

In addition, ATF needs to improve its sharing of firearms-trafficking related information and techniques within its intelligence structure. ATF Southwest border intelligence personnel need to more routinely exchange information, analytical techniques, and best practices within and across field divisions.

ATF also needs to revisit its implementation of a key component of Project Gunrunner – the Border Liaison Program. We found that the liaisons need to coordinate their cross-border activities between their own field divisions and ATF's Mexico Country Office and need their roles more clearly defined.

Project Gunrunner's investigative focus has largely remained on gun dealer inspections and straw purchaser investigations, rather than targeting higher-level traffickers and smugglers. As a result, ATF has not made full use of the intelligence, technological, and prosecutorial resources that can help ATF's investigations reach into the higher levels of trafficking rings.

ATF also needs to make better use of the OCDETF Program, to target the higher levels of firearms trafficking rings.

ATF did not effectively implement Project Gunrunner as a multi-agency program. Despite the existence of an MOU between ATF and ICE, collaboration between the agencies, which share jurisdiction over firearms trafficking, must be improved. ATF needs to provide supplemental guidance to field supervisors on the coordination of pertinent and necessary information in areas of concurrent jurisdiction between ATF and ICE.

ATF is unable to generate timely, actionable intelligence on suspected firearms traffickers, in part because it cannot obtain accurate crime gun trace data from Mexico. Many crime guns seized in Mexico are not traced, and the percentage of traces successfully conducted is low and declining. Even when traces succeed, the results are often untimely and cannot be used to generate investigative leads. ATF needs to more effectively communicate ATF's Project Gunrunner strategy and the successes from tracing information provided by Mexican agencies, to Mexican law enforcement authorities.

ATF has been unable to respond to many training, support and information requests from government of Mexico agencies, and does not have the staff it requires at its Mexico Country Office to fully do so. Nor has ATF fully integrated the activities of its Southwest border field divisions and the Mexico Country Office. ATF needs a better information sharing and intelligence capability in its Mexico Country Office and to integrate activities with the Southwest border field divisions.

In this report, we make 15 recommendations to ATF to help improve their efforts to combat firearms trafficking from the United States to Mexico. Specifically, we recommend that ATF:

1. Coordinate with the government of Mexico, the CBP, DEA and ICE to ensure systematic and regular exchanges of strategic intelligence to combat firearms trafficking to Mexico.

2. Work with the Department to explore options for seeking a requirement for reporting multiple sales of long guns.

3. Ensure that each Southwest border firearms trafficking enforcement group develops and regularly updates general guidelines for their Field Intelligence Group to follow that specify the most useful types of investigative leads.

4. Develop an automated process that enables ATF managers to track and evaluate the usefulness of investigative leads provided to firearms trafficking enforcement groups.

5. Develop and implement procedures for Southwest border intelligence personnel to routinely exchange intelligence-related information in accordance with ATF Order 3700.2A and the Intelligence Collection Plan.

6. Develop a method for Southwest border intelligence personnel to regularly share analytical techniques and best practices pertaining to Project Gunrunner.

7. Formalize a position description that establishes minimum expectations regarding the roles and responsibilities of border liaisons.

8. Focus on developing more complex conspiracy cases against higher level gun traffickers and gun trafficking conspirators.

9. Send guidance to field management, agents, and intelligence staff encouraging them to participate in and exploit the resources and tools of the OCDETF Program, as directed in the Deputy Attorney General's cartel strategy.

10. Provide guidance to ATF field supervisors and agents to better coordinate with ICE, including direction on how to "coordinate all pertinent and necessary information" in areas of "concurrent jurisdiction," as defined in the memorandum of understanding.

11. Work with the government of Mexico to determine the causes of unsuccessful traces and develop actions to improve the rate of successful traces.

12. Regularly and more effectively communicate ATF's Project Gunrunner strategy to Mexican law enforcement authorities, including the value of gun tracing and the successes involving information or tracing information provided by Mexican agencies.

13. Develop better information sharing and intelligence analysis capability at its Mexico Country Office.

14. In coordination with the Mexico Attorney General's office, evaluate the mutual benefits, roles, and information sharing protocols of the Mexico Attorney General's office representative pilot program to determine whether to expand the program to each of ATF's Southwest border field divisions.

15. Ensure that the reforms discussed in ATF's September 2010 "Project Gunrunner – A Cartel Focused Strategy" are fully and expeditiously implemented.

APPENDIX I: TIMELINE OF KEY PROJECT GUNRUNNER EVENTS

Year	Month	Activity
2005	June	Project Gunrunner pilot project in Laredo, Texas.
2006	April	Project Gunrunner official launch date.
2008	January	Expanded Project Gunrunner by adding 58 staff to the Southwest border field divisions, 3 additional staff to EPIC, and deploying eTrace to all U.S. consulates in Mexico.
	June	Merida Initiative signed into law, allocated $2 million to expand Spanish eTrace throughout Mexico and Central America.
2009	February	The Recovery Act signed into law, allocated $10 million to ATF for Project Gunrunner.
	March	White House announced enhanced action at the Southwest border and the relocation of 100 personnel to the Southwest border for 120 days via Gun Runner Impact Teams.
	June	Supplemental Appropriations Act of 2009 allocated an additional $6 million to ATF for Project Gunrunner.
	September	New Gunrunner Teams established in El Centro, California; McAllen, Texas; and Las Cruces and Roswell, New Mexico.
	December	Spanish eTrace piloted in Mexico.
2010	June (In progress)	Deploy Spanish eTrace to Mexican state police laboratories.
	August	Emergency Border Security Supplemental Appropriations Bill of 2010 allocated $37.5 million to ATF for Project Gunrunner.
	September (Anticipated)	Hiring of 37 new staff with Recovery Act funds to be completed (89% complete as of June 2010).
		New ATF offices in the U.S. consulates in Tijuana and Juarez (75% complete as of June 2010).

The information below was obtained from ATF's official position descriptions and interviews with ATF staff.

Special Agent (agent) federal law enforcement officers who generally investigates criminal violations of federal laws that fall under the jurisdiction of ATF such as arson and explosive cases, convicted felon in possession of a gun, alcohol and tobacco crimes, and firearms trafficking. They contribute to Project Gunrunner by investigating crimes linked to firearms trafficking to Mexico, securing indictments from the Assistant United States Attorneys, and arresting the individuals. Such crimes include guns acquired by straw purchasers, corrupt gun dealers, and conspiracy firearms trafficking cases.

Industry Operations Investigator generally conducts inspections of new gun dealers and federal explosives licensees by reviewing records, inventory, and the licensee's conduct of business. They are also responsible for training gun dealers on the relevant laws as well as detecting and preventing firearms trafficking by noticing indicators and suspicious behaviors. Industry Operations Investigators have an important role in Project Gunrunner to educate gun dealers to avoid selling guns to suspected firearms traffickers, provide intelligence and make referrals to ATF agents when suspected firearms trafficking activity is taking place, and assist with the analysis of gun dealers and the records they keep.

Intelligence Research Specialist performs in-depth intelligence analyses in support of ATF operations. They provide intelligence products such as link analyses, visual investigative analyses, and telephone toll record analyses to provide ATF staff with information about ongoing or emerging investigations. Intelligence Research Specialists also act in liaison and coordination functions both within ATF (with headquarters and other field offices) as well as with external partners, such as other federal law enforcement.

Investigative Analyst functions in an investigative and research support position for ATF which includes compiling information from ATF databases on criminal leads and compiling reports for the use of ATF staff. Investigative Analysts also perform many of the administrative functions for an enforcement group or field office.

Area Supervisor typically manages a group of about 10 Industry Operations Investigators, although these Industry Operations Investigators are frequently dispersed throughout satellite offices. In addition to managing, hiring, and training, an area supervisor assigns Industry Operations Investigators to inspect gun dealers as well as explosive dealers and, when needed, receives referrals for criminal investigations from Industry Operations Investigators and passes them on to the intelligence group.

Group Supervisor typically manages a group of about 10 agents who comprise an enforcement group. He or she provides guidance and supervision for criminal investigations and distributes work to these agents, often based on referrals from intelligence and industry operations. A group supervisor can also be called a "resident agent in charge" when the head of an enforcement group located in a city that is not the field division headquarters.

Director of Industry Operations is in charge of all the Industry Operations Investigators and area supervisors within a field division. He or she determines where to locate staff within the field division and decides which gun dealers are inspected, usually based on the time since the last compliance inspection.

APPENDIX III: INTERVIEWS

Organization/Division	Position
ATF Interviews	
ATF Headquarters	Chief, Firearms Programs Division, Office of Field Operations
	Chief, Firearms Operations Division, Office of Field Operations
	Chief, Criminal Intelligence Division, OSII
	Field Intelligence Support Branch, Criminal Intelligence Division, OSII (x4)
	Program Manager, N-FOCIS Branch
	Chief, Office of International Affairs
	Chief of Staff, Office of Training and Professional Development
	Staff member, Special Operations Division
	Deputy Assistant Director, Field Operations (West)
National Tracing Center	Chief, and Deputy Chief, National Tracing Center
	Branch Chief, Law Enforcement Support Branch
	Supervisory Analyst, Information Systems Analysis Group
	Branch Chief, Industry Records Branch
	Program Analyst, Firearms Tracing Branch, International Trace Section
Violent Crime Analysis Branch	Branch Chief
Los Angeles Field Division	Special Agent in Charge
	Assistant Special Agent in Charge (x2)
	Director of Industry Operations
	Area Supervisor
	Industry Operations Investigator
	Field Intelligence Group Supervisor
	Intelligence Research Specialist
	Industry Operations Intelligence Specialist
	Tracing Specialist, Regional Crime Gun Center
	Group Supervisor, Glendale
	Resident Agent in Charge, San Diego
	Resident Agent in Charge, El Centro
	Special Agent, Glendale
	Special Agent, San Diego
	Border Liaison Officer
Phoenix Field Division	Special Agent in Charge
	Assistant Special Agent in Charge (x2)
	Director of Industry Operations
	Area Supervisor (x2)
	Field Intelligence Group Supervisor
	Intelligence Research Specialist/e-Trace Coordinator
	Intelligence Agent, Field Intelligence Group
	Group Supervisor
	Special Agent (x2)
Dallas Field Division	Special Agent in Charge

Organization/Division	Position
	Assistant Special Agent in Charge (x2)
	Director of Industry Operations
	Area Supervisor
	Field Intelligence Group Supervisor
	Intelligence Research Specialist
	Industry Operations Intelligence Specialist
	Group Supervisor, Dallas
	Group Supervisor, Fort Worth
	Special Agent (x4)
Mexico Country Office	Attaché to Mexico
	Assistant Attaché (x2)
	Special Agent
	Intelligence Research Specialist
	Foreign Service National (x4)
Non-ATF Interviews	
Drug Enforcement Administration	Staff Coordinator, Operations Division, Office of Global Enforcement, Mexico and Central America Section
	Mexico-Central America Intelligence Unit Chief, DEA Office of Strategic Intelligence
	Assistant Special Agent in Charge, Los Angeles Field Division
	Assistant Special Agent in Charge, Phoenix Field Division
	Assistant Special Agent in Charge, Dallas Field Division
	Regional Director, Mexico and Central America Division, Mexico City, Mexico
Immigration and Custom Enforcement Headquarters	Chief, Office of Investigations, Contraband Smuggling Unit; Program Manager, Operation Armas Cruzadas
	Assistant Special Agent in Charge, Los Angeles Field Division
	Special Agent in Charge, Phoenix Field Division
	Special Agent, Dallas Field Division
	Deputy Attaché, Mexico City, Mexico
Customs and Border Protection Headquarters	Director, International Affairs Office; International Affairs Officer, International Affairs Office; Program Manager, Office of Field Operations; Assistant Chief, Southwest Border Division, Office of Border Patrol; Officer, Office of Border Patrol; Policy Advisor, Office of Policy and Planning; Liaison, Office of Air and Marine; Liaison, Office of International Affairs; Liaison, Office of Border Patrol; Liaison, Office of Training and Development
	Acting Assistant Director, Border Security, Los Angeles Field Office
	Lead Border Patrol Agent, U.S. Border Patrol, Marfa Sector Intelligence, Sierra Blanca, Texas
	Special Operations Supervisor, Canine Unit, El Paso, Texas
	Assistant Director for Border Security, U.S. Customs and Border Patrol, Tucson, Arizona
	Yuma Sector Chief, U.S. Border Patrol

Organization/Division	Position
	Attaché and Assistant Attaché to Mexico
Executive Office for United States Attorneys	Project Safe Neighborhoods National Coordinator
U.S. Attorney's Office for the Central District of California	Project Safe Neighborhood/Assistant United States Attorney; Assistant United States Attorney
U.S. Attorney's Office for the Northern District of Texas	Deputy Criminal Chief
U.S. Attorney's Office for the Eastern District of Texas	Assistant United States Attorney
U.S. Attorney's Office for Arizona	United States Attorney for Arizona and Assistant United States Attorney
Criminal Division	Deputy Assistant Attorney General
International Affairs Office	Department of Justice Attaché to Mexico
Office of Overseas Prosecutorial Development, Assistance, and Training	Chief and Deputy Chief
Department of State	U.S. Ambassador to Mexico; Deputy Chief of Mission, U.S. Embassy in Mexico City
	Merida Coordinator, Bureau of International Narcotics and Law Enforcement Affairs
	Deputy Director and Drug Interdiction Program Coordinator, Narcotics Affairs Section, Mexico City, Mexico
	Assistant Regional Security Officer, Mexico City, Mexico
Government Accountability Office	GAO Analyst-In-Charge, International Affairs Section, Washington DC
Mexican Government Interviews	
Mexican Military	Senior Officers
PGR	Assistant Attorney General for Special Investigations and Organized Crime, representatives from the Special Unit for Investigation into Crimes Against Health and the Special Unit for Investigation of Terrorism, Arms Stockpiling and Trafficking.
PGR-CENAPI	Director of CENAPI along with representatives from the General Analysis Against Crime, Office of International Analysis, Office of Weapons and Armed Groups, Office of Information against Kidnappings and other Crimes, Directorate of Firearms and Explosives.
	PGR-CENAPI Representative to ATF Phoenix Field Division
Secretariat of Public Security	Representative from the International Affairs Office (x2)
Mexican Secretariat of Foreign Affairs	Representative from the Directorate of North America (x2)

Phoenix	• Developed a strategy of intelligence-lead policing whereby the Field Intelligence Group will analyze and disseminate leads, as the point of contact for other field divisions and agencies.
	• Two agents each dedicated full time to the Phoenix and Tucson OCDETF.
	• Border liaison officers in Phoenix, Tucson, and Yuma, Arizona.
	• Embedded a representative from the Mexico Attorney General's office (CENAPI).*
	• Conducted a conference call with Los Angeles and San Francisco Field Divisions.
	• Industry Operations would target high-risk gun dealers for inspections based on risk factors found through intelligence.
Dallas	• Field Intelligence Group will coordinate trafficking intelligence to appropriate field offices, within ATF including the Mexico Country Office and Southwest border Field Intelligence Groups, and other law enforcement.
	• Field Intelligence Group will be the conduit between law enforcement and Industry Operations, with regular collaboration between the two.
	• Border liaison officer in El Paso, Texas.
	• Due to close proximity to the border, agents work closely with other federal agencies (DEA and ICE) and local police.
	• Train and coordinate U.S. Attorneys and local prosecutors, to ensure that cases are successfully prosecuted.
	• Industry Operations will conduct focused inspections on gun dealers who show indicators of firearms trafficking.
Los Angeles	• Field Intelligence Group will analyze information and leads to assign to field offices for investigation.
	• Conference calls will be conducted between the Los Angeles, San Francisco, and Phoenix field divisions for coordination and information sharing between field divisions.
	• Border liaison officer in San Diego, California.
	• Firearms trafficking group (San Diego I) works with local law enforcement, ICE, the FBI, and through the border liaison, Mexican law enforcement
	• Will coordinate with U.S. Attorneys and county District Attorneys to address issues in cases so fast and successful prosecutions can occur

* The representative from the Mexico Attorney General's office was a pilot program that was to be evaluated in summer 2010.